Taking Stock

Journalism and the Publicly Traded
Newspaper Company

Taking Stock

Journalism and the Publicly Traded Newspaper Company

Gilbert Cranberg
George H. Gallup Professor of Journalism, Emeritus

Randall Bezanson
Charles E. Floete Distinguished Professor of Law

John Soloski
Daniel and Amy Starch Professor
Director, School of Journalism
and Mass Communication

Iowa State University Press / Ames

©Copyright 2001 Iowa State University Press
All rights reserved

Iowa State University Press
2121 South State Avenue, Ames, Iowa 50014

Orders: 1-800-862-6657
Office: 1-515-292-0140
Fax: 515-292-3348
Web site (secure): www.isupress.com

Authorization to photocopy items for internal or personal use, or the internal or personal use of specific clients, is granted by Iowa State University Press, provided that the base fee of $.10 per copy is paid directly to the Copyright Clearance Center, 222 Rosewood Drive, Danvers, MA 01923. For those organizations that have been granted a photocopy license by CCC, a separate system of payments has been arranged. The fee code for users of the Transactional Reporting Service is 0-8138-2459-1/01$.10.

Printed on acid-free paper from camera-ready copy provided by the authors

First edition, 2001

Library of Congress Cataloging-in-Publication Data

Cranberg, Gilbert
    Taking stock: journalism and the publicly traded newspaper company/Gilbert Cranberg, Randall Bezanson, John Soloski. – 1st ed.
    p. cm.
Includes bibliographical references and index.
ISBN 0-8138-2459-1 (alk. paper)
    1. American newspapers—Ownership. 2. Newspaper publishing—United States—History-20th Century. I. Bezanson, Randall. II. Soloski, John. III. Title.

PN488.085 C73 2001   2001016996
338.4'70713–dc21

The last digit is the print number: 9 8 7 6 5 4 3 2 1

Contents

Preface and Acknowledgments vii

Chapter I Introduction 1

    A. Methodology 3
    B. Summary of Conclusions 6

**Chapter II The Publicly Held Newspaper
               Corporation, 2000** 17

    A. The Newspaper Business 17
    B. An Overview of Publicly Traded Newspaper
        Companies 25
    C. Financial Performance 33

Chapter III Ownership and Control 41

    A. Boards of Directors 41
    B. Ownership Structure 43
    C. Investment-oriented Management 52
    D. The Influence of the Investment Community:
        Analysts 56
    E. The CEO's 64
    F. The Omnipresence of the Investment Market 72

Chapter IV Organizational Behavior and Dynamics in the Publicly Traded Newspaper Firm 77

    A. Introduction 77
    B. The Editors 77
    C. Circulation 90
    D. The Shape of the Firm 98
    E. The New Newspaper Enterprise 107

Chapter V The Changed Economic and Competitive Environment: Technology and the New Economics of News 115

    A. Economics and the Emergence of the Newspaper 116
    B. Changing Economic and Technological Forces at Mid-Century 122
    C. The New Economic Imperatives of News: The Atomization of News and the Newspaper 125

Chapter VI Fettering Capitalism: Some Recommendations 135

    A. Is Change Possible or Desirable? 135
        1. The Role of Economic Forces 135
        2. Are We Simply Getting What We Want? ... 138
    B. Recommendations for Change 141
    C. Conclusion 153

Appendix A Company Information 155

Appendix B Account of the June 1999 Mid-Year Media Review 197

Index 201

Preface and Acknowledgments

This book is the end product of a study undertaken with financial support from the Open Society Institute of New York, which awarded us Individual Project Fellowship grants.

The study grew out of our sense that the dissatisfactions with the quality of journalism that were being increasingly voiced in the mid-1990s reflected more than the commonly cited complaints about newsroom staffing, newspaper content, and the like. More fundamental forces appeared to be at work, forces operating on the news firm itself, and indeed on the organization and incentives built into the very definition of the firm and its purposes.

We concluded that, because of their reach and influence, the publicly traded newspaper companies were a logical focus for study. They are a relatively recent phenomenon; the first newspaper company to "go public," Dow Jones, did so less than 40 years ago. An important consideration, moreover, is that due to disclosure requirements the information necessary to the study of a newspaper firm and its operation was most likely to be available for the public firms.

The study involved many people and drew upon many disciplines, from journalism to business to social science to law. The University of Iowa proved (unsurprisingly to us) an extremely comfortable and encouraging place to engage in work that crosses disciplines. For this we are grateful. The University also made it possible to work with a large group of very talented students. From Journalism and Mass Communications we had the valuable research assistance of Heather Baker, Vanessa Carney, Lisa Creger, Mia Consalvo, Gene Costain, Douglas Frederick, Brian Graves, Mark Johns, Janella Newsome, Tracy Potocki, Jennifer Tiernan, Andy Toh, Anna Vorm, Greg Wallace, and James Wolf. From the College of Law we had the able assistance of Jamie Clanton, Jake Curtis, Jennifer Gates, Dan Harmelink, and David Peters. Valuable assistance was provided by Hsun-Chih Kuo of the Statistical Consulting Center at the University of Iowa. Coordinating the efforts of the students and, in the end, assembling the many fragments into a coherent whole was a job made infinitely easier by two able assistants, Susan Troyer in the Law School, and Connie Davis in Journalism and Mass Communications. Finally, we would be remiss in not giving special thanks to the many executives, editors, journalists, stock analysts, and others in the newspaper industry who spoke with us.

Thanks also are due Iowa State University Press for its eagerness to publish the study as a book and to expedite its publication.

Taking Stock

Journalism and the Publicly Traded
Newspaper Company

Chapter I

Introduction

News is a business. It has always been so. It was so in England, where the hated Stamp Act made it impossible to distribute news profitably to a wide and general audience, and where the eventual elimination of the stamp allowed the cheap mass newspapers, large and small, rural and urban, to thrive and expand. It was so in America where, unsaddled by the Stamp Act and enlivened by public demand for news, the 19th Century witnessed the emergence and growth of the highly profitable penny press and the great metropolitan newspapers. It is no accident that the newspaper as we know it is a product of capitalism and private enterprise. The search for profit yielded newspapers of increasingly broad, mass distribution, oriented to the public interest in information, and freed of any obligation to the patronizing demands of class or to duties imposed by government. Business has been good for news. Its private capitalist impulse created a broadly democratic, public, and fiercely independent newspaper.

The business of news is news. The growth of the newspaper industry in America has been driven by the public's appetite for news, for information of current moment upon which people in communities and in a nation could make political, social, and economic decisions, large and small. As the United States Supreme Court has put it, news provides information and opinion that "enable[s] the members of society to cope with the exigencies of their period."[1] News was the product around which the business was shaped. The news was selected, presented, and packaged in appealing and therefore profitable ways, to be sure, but the central focus of the newspaper has been the publication of news.

---

[1] Rosenbloom v. Metromedia, 403 U.S. 29, 41 (1971); Curtis Pub. Co. v. Butts, 388 U.S. 130, 148 (1967); quoting Thornhill v. Alabama, 310 U.S. 88, 102 (1940).

Dramatic change is now afoot, however. Today, the business of news is business, not news. This trend is strikingly revealed in the news produced by the publicly owned newspaper companies, which account for over 40 percent of the daily newspaper circulation, and over 50 percent of the Sunday circulation, in the United States. For these companies, it seems, news is no longer the focus of the newspaper, the central product around which all else revolves. Instead, news has become secondary, even incidental, to markets and revenues and margins and advertisers and consumer preferences. The business of news is no longer the providing of broad public information to a mass public audience, but the providing of specialized information, formats, and angles to smaller and smaller, and more and more profitable, audiences. News is shaped by the audience, rather than the audience being shaped by the news.

When the publicly held newspaper companies are combined with the newspaper chains that are not publicly held, the large newspaper organizations today account for about 75 percent of the daily circulation. And they are expanding rapidly. Having early on penetrated the large-circulation markets, and then having moved on to the medium to small markets, chains are now acquiring large numbers of newspapers serving the smallest-circulation markets in small towns throughout the country. The publicly traded segment of the newspaper business includes firms with varied commitment to quality journalism, and their papers range from distinguished to undistinguished. However varied, the firms share a common feature: They are subject to the unceasing demands of the investment marketplace, populated by individuals, corporations, institutional investors, and other passive investors, large and small, whose interest is profits and margins and yields and share value; whose interest, in short, is business, not news.

This is not to imply that the privately held newspaper company is a preferable form of ownership. Individually and collectively, there may or may not be significant differences between papers owned by private and public companies. We venture no opinion, because our purpose was not to draw comparisons. Rather, it was to draw a picture of this relatively new force in journalism.

While the publicly traded companies are the instruments of

fundamental change in the newspaper industry in the United States, they are not, however, the cause of change. They are instead simply manifestations of larger and structural forces at work. Our aim in this study is to understand the changes taking place in the newspaper business, the role being played by the publicly owned newspaper companies, and the structural economic, market, and technological forces that govern them. Our aim, in short, is both descriptive and analytical, focused specifically on the organization and behavior and business practices of the publicly held newspaper company. If changes are driven by structural forces, and if some of those changes are undesirable, it is of no use to focus criticism on specific companies or to admonish individuals to change their ways. Structural change requires structural responses.

A. Methodology

We began our study in 1997. Over the following two years we assembled a very large body of information upon which to base our study. The information ranged from specific information about the companies we selected for study, to information about the financial markets in which their securities are traded and the institutional investors that own large stakes in those securities, to information about the economic, legal, and technological environments in which the newspaper companies operate.

The companies we chose to study are the major publicly held companies that own daily newspapers. In varying degrees these companies, of course, own other media (and sometimes non-media) businesses, but in combination the companies' newspapers account for 40-50 percent of the daily newspaper circulation in the United States. The 17 companies we selected for study are:

A. H. Belo Corporation
Central Newspapers
Dow Jones & Company
E. W. Scripps Company
Gannett Company
Gray Communications Systems
Hollinger International
Journal Register Company
Knight Ridder, Inc.
Lee Enterprises
The McClatchy Company
Media General, Inc.
The New York Times Company
Pulitzer Publishing Company
The Times Mirror Company
Tribune Company
The Washington Post Company

The companies are businesses in flux. When we initiated our study in 1997, Times Mirror and Central Newspapers were separate entities but have since been acquired. Since then, Hollinger has sold many newspaper properties, Journal Register said it would shed its Midwest papers, and Lee Enterprises sold broadcast properties. Thus, any detailed description of the newspaper business is a snapshot. The picture in this volume was snapped as of 1999. While there has been change in the companies, there has not necessarily been a change in the phenomena we identify.

For each company we compiled a broad array of information, including:

- Detailed current and historical financial information;

- Information about stock price and performance over time;

- Information about the distribution of stock ownership by board members, management, institutional investors and, where applicable, family members;

- Information about the organizational structure, management, corporate policies, compensation arrangements, and executive officers of the holding companies;

- Information, as available, about the profitability, performance, strategic plans, circulation, and organization and operation of the subsidiary operating newspapers;

- Interviews with more than 100 editors, copy editors, CEO's, and stock analysts who follow newspaper companies.

Much of the detailed financial, operating, and organizational information about the companies was obtained from published annual reports to shareholders, from reports to the Securities Exchange Commission, and from proxy material. Institutional investor and other stock-ownership information was also generally available from these sources as well as from standard financial services, such as Vickers. Circulation information was obtained from published industry-wide studies or from specific reports compiled for use by the industry. Advertising, revenue, and other information was obtained through sources that compile such information for companies' use, or occasionally from the operating newspapers themselves.

General information about the economics of the newspaper industry, the economics of communication, technological changes, and social and cultural forces influencing newspaper readership was obtained from published sources in the fields of business, economics, communication, journalism, law, and sociology. Material related to the legal forces bearing on the publicly held newspaper company, including changes in the regulation of securities and securities markets, was compiled by researchers at the Iowa Law School.

We also were assisted by the interesting and insightful case studies that were being published during the course of our research by the project entitled "The State of the American Newspaper," as well as by other projects such as the "Newspaper Credibility Project" of the American Society of Newspaper Editors (ASNE) and the Project for Excellence in Journalism. In many ways the "State of the American Newspaper" project parallels our project, but the relationship between the projects is complementary, not competing. The "State of the American Newspaper" project focuses on identifying changes in the newspaper business through detailed and thematic case studies, leading to an understanding of the operating practices and philosophy of specific newspapers and companies. Our study is focused on a more systematic understanding of structural forces–economic, market, social, legal, and technological–that are shaping the daily newspaper industry, with a specific emphasis on that part of the industry owned by publicly held newspaper/communications companies. Theirs is a microeconomic assessment; our is a more macroeconomic one.

Our focus, of course, is also on the newspaper companies, and specifically on such matters as stock-market influence, strategic plans and priorities, the composition of boards of directors and executive management, operating arrangements and controls over the subsidiary newspaper companies, compensation policies and practices, revenue and cost and circulation objectives and results, and so forth. But we look at such matters at the level of the firm and across an industry group, rather than through individual case studies. And we are trying to understand the forces that account for the practices and behaviors we find, so that we can determine whether there are feasible solutions to the problems we or others identify, and offer recommendations.

B. Summary of Conclusions

We conclude that the American newspaper is undergoing fundamental change, and that the change is compromising the newspaper's continued role as a fiercely independent source of information and opinion judged relevant and necessary for public understanding in a free, democratic, capitalist society.

- The publicly traded newspaper companies are a major, though not the only, force in producing this change. Economic forces, driven by technology, have contributed substantially to the changes that are taking place. The economics of printing and distribution have shortened the news cycle, even for newspapers, and have made market segmentation and content specialization both possible and, more important, profitable. Technology has broken down old market divisions and is rapidly creating new ones. The newspaper is having to redefine its character, even its soul.

- But the publicly traded newspaper company adds something new, something very powerful, and something that is not economically or technologically predestined, to the equation. That something is (i) widely distributed ownership, (ii) in a highly competitive and liquid financial marketplace, by (iii) persons and institutions whose interests are strictly financial and whose expectations are by definition short term because of easy access to alternative investments at a moment's notice. The stock market, in short, represents the owners of the newspaper companies and thus dictates the behavior of the companies pervasively and at all levels of the organization.
- Ownership of the companies by thousands of passive investors interested in financial return, not news quality, has distorted the direction of change caused by economic and technological forces, and thus the capacity of newspapers to continue to perform their historic and constitutionally protected role as the foundation of a free press.

- Investors in the firms are concerned with revenues, margins, continuously improving profitability, and stock performance. They are indifferent to news or, more disturbingly, its quality. This is especially the case with the large institutional investors that control, on average, 50 percent of the traded shares of the publicly traded companies.
- The publicly traded newspaper companies have been "incentivized" from top to bottom in order to assure that policies, decisions, and corporate behaviors conform to the performance demands of the securities markets.
- Executive management and Board members are directly responsible to the owners, and therefore to the demands of the stock market and the institutional investors who may own a substantial portion of the company's stock. Both board and executive compensation are highly "market incentivized," often consisting principally of bonuses based on market performance and forms of stock option that are dependent on stock performance.
- The publishers, editors, and other members of the operating newspaper companies' management, as well as key editorial and news personnel, are also frequently compensated by a combination of profit- and margin-based bonuses and stock options, or both, with the bonus and option packages often comprising a third to a half or even more of the recipient's annual income. Employees responsible for the operation of the newspaper companies are thus incentivized to achieve the market-based objectives set by the board and corporate executive management.

- For the public companies (with but few exceptions), the business of news is business, not news. Their papers are managed and controlled for financial performance, not news quality.
- Central corporate control over operating newspapers is rarely focused on news content; it is instead strictly financial, measured by such neutral criteria as revenue growth, operating margins, advertising rates, and the like. But it is understood by all that financial controls enforced by the parent company compel known changes in size and quality of editorial staff, content, newshole, priorities for coverage, market segmentation, etc.
- The principal objective of the newspaper companies is revenue growth and margin. Circulation often is of secondary consequence, and then only if increased circulation can yield increased profit margins.
- The most important revenue source is advertising, and newspaper behavior increasingly reflects an eagerness to respond to the need for increased advertising revenue and rates.
- The most important short-term strategy for increasing margins is cutting costs, and this consists principally of cutting personnel. News personnel are often seen as not contributing to revenues or margins, and are therefore cut heavily.
- Markets are being consciously segmented in order to deliver readers, who are often seen as eyeballs for advertisers. Segmentation occurs along many lines, but socioeconomic segmentation has been the most favored, for with a socioeconomically wealthy market

- advertising efficiency, and thus advertising rates, can be increased.
- Competition for socioeconomically defined market segments increasingly takes the form of altering the subject matter and shape of news content, delivering the types and forms of information that persons in the socioeconomically defined market prefer. The independence of the newspaper, not from government but from unvarnished consumer preferences, is thus jeopardized.
- Operating margins, which have historically been in the 10 to 15 percent range for newspapers, now range between 20 and 30 percent and higher in the newspapers owned by the public companies.
- A few of the public companies have managed, so far at least, to blunt the financial-market forces that increasingly govern the behavior of the rest of the firms. Prominent among these few exceptions to the rule are the McClatchy Newspapers, The Washington Post Company, and (at least for their flagship newspapers) the New York Times Company and Dow Jones. These companies each have sufficient family ownership, combined in one case with a long-term institutional investor, to take the long view with respect to corporate policies and returns, and not to be driven by the compulsion of constantly improving quarterly or even annual financial performance.
- Because the publicly traded companies control such a large segment of the newspaper industry, because they have such vast resources, and because they continue to acquire private and independent newspapers, their practices and their priorities and their

standards are becoming the standards to which all newspapers must subscribe in order to survive.

- At the level of the firm, changes in newspaper operations and in the quality and character of the news product reflect a combination of two interrelated forces: size of the organization and the resulting forms of management and control; and the hydraulic and strictly financial and investment-based forces exerted by the stock market.

—Size has resulted in often decentralized control over editorial content, but within the framework of very strict and increasingly aggressive financial controls that constrain choices about content and introduce new incentives into the operating newspapers. More recently many of the public companies, have begun to seek advantages from grouping papers into dominant metropolitan and regional chains and then combining many aspects of news operations and sharing news among all of the nominally separate papers. This is a strategy of vertical integration through control over content.

—Stock-market pressures have exacerbated the emphasis on revenue, margins, profits, and stock-price performance, forcing the companies to emphasize the aspects of newspaper operation that directly produce those results: lean staffing, low salaries, efficiency, orientation to advertiser preferences, definition of market and audience in terms of advertising-revenue yield, de-emphasis on mass audiences, de-emphasis on circulation revenues and increased emphasis on advertising revenues.

There are a number of consequences for news and news quality that have or are likely to result from these changes. They are:

- Reduction in the quantity and quality of newsroom staff risks a reduction in quality assurance and accuracy.
- Breaking down the organizational separation between news and business that has traditionally marked newspaper companies, with the result that news judgments will end to enjoy less independence in the organizational structure of the firm.
- The introduction of stock-price and financial incentives in the compensation of editorial personnel in the newspaper, which over time may compromise the independence of news judgments from financial self-interest and the firm's strictly financial objectives.
- A changed definition of the audience for news, from a public audience to an advertiser-driven "market" defined by socioeconomic characteristics and consumer buying habits.
- Changes in the format, substance, and emphasis of newspaper content that are geared to the newly defined market audience, and thus a likely change in the orientation of news judgment from information and opinion that is important to the public to material that is preferred by a market.
- Because of strict financial controls, less flexibility is enjoyed in making judgments about coverage of news, including the newspaper's ability to develop and stay with potentially important stories whose yield is uncertain.
- Because of increased monopoly power in small and large newspaper markets, public or

audience needs may be given less weight when resolving conflicts among business or advertiser interests and subscriber and community interest.

- Because of increased monopoly presence of large newspaper organizations on a local, regional, and state level, and because of the more recent trend toward vertical integration through the acquisition of all papers in selected markets by a single firm, fewer resources are being committed by competing newspapers to coverage of politics, state government, and business affairs.[2] Readers are becoming increasingly dependent on single- or limited- source news, especially at the local level.[3]

- Because of increasing concentration of newspapers in the hands of large companies, competition among newspapers based on the quality of news is diminishing. The terms of competition have little or nothing to do with news quality–the quality of the product produced by the firm–in most markets today.

* * *

Based on these and other conclusions, which are explained and developed in greater detail in the pages that follow, we offer a

---

[2] Project for Excellence in Journalism, *Changing Definitions of News: A Look at the Mainstream Press Over 20 Years* (1998); *Examining Our Credibility: Why Newspaper Credibility Has Been Dropping*, Journ. Credibility Project, ASNE. (1998).

[3] Charles Layton and Mary Walton, "Missing the Story at the Statehouse," *American Journalism Review*, July/August 1998, pp. 42-63, *http://ajr.newslink.org/special/part3.html*.

number of possible avenues for change, recommendations that might relieve the relentless pressure of the markets and its corroding influence on the quality of news in the papers owned by the publicly traded newspaper companies. Chief among our recommendations are these:

- Prohibition of incentive compensation in the form of stock options or grants, and prohibition of other forms of incentive compensation (including bonuses) based predominantly on financial performance, for the editors and news staff of the operating newspaper companies.
- Restrictions on the proportion of compensation for executive management (including newspaper publishers) based only on financial performance, coupled with the creation of new incentives based not on market performance of the stock, but instead on expanding circulation and on the quality of journalism practiced in the company's newspapers.
- Dramatic changes in the composition and allegiance of boards of directors of public newspaper companies, such as a strict limit on the number of inside board members, a prohibition on the awarding of stock options and market-based incentives to board members, and express legal authorization for boards to consider news quality and the community's interest in its newspaper's mission when making all decisions, even when the maximization of short-term shareholder return is compromised.
- Changes in tax and securities laws that would encourage long-term investment in newspaper companies, such as a greatly lengthened

holding period in order to receive capital gains tax treatment, and other incentives that would attract long term investors to newspaper stocks.[4]

The recommendations are directed at blunting both day-to-day operating incentives and the larger, structural market forces that are reshaping the newspaper companies from those whose business is news into those whose business is business.

---

[4] Notably, a step in this direction has recently been taken with a general reduction in capital gains rates from 20 to 18 percent for investments held for five years or longer.

Chapter II

The Publicly Held Newspaper Corporation, 2000

There has always been tension between the business and journalistic sides of newspapers. As a business, newspapers need to earn profits. However, the drive for profits can come at the expense of journalistic quality. It is an age-old question in journalism whether newspapers earn profits to invest in journalism, or whether they earn profits to make owners and investors richer. Some newspaper owners long ago decided the answer. Lord Thompson once said: "I buy newspapers to make money to buy newspapers to make money. As for editorial content, that's the stuff you separate the ads with."[5]

A. The Newspaper Business

Today, the newspaper industry finds itself in an environment marked by increased competition for advertising and subscription dollars. It is an environment unlike any before in communication, in that readers have more choices for how to spend their news and entertainment dollars. The Internet promises to increase this competition.

The environment is also one where investment dollars reside primarily in the hands of large institutions, such as mutual funds, investment banks, insurance companies, pension funds, and colleges and universities.[6] In the past 20 years, institutional investors have

---

[5] Quoted in Ben H. Bagdikian, *Newspaper mergers – the Final Phase*, Columbia Journalism Review, March/April 1977, p. 21.

[6] John Soloski and Robert Picard, "The New Media Lords: Why Institutional Investors Call the Shots," *Columbia Journalism*

become the dominant holders of equities in U.S. companies. By necessity, many of these investors tend to focus on the short-term business and market performance of their investments. A short-term market orientation can limit the ability of companies owned by investors to engage in long-term planning, for management must focus on meeting the short-term results expected by institutional investors.

Over the past 10 or so years investors in newspaper companies have generally done well. Despite increased competition and declines in circulation, readership, and the number of dailies, the newspaper industry continues to thrive economically.

In 1997, for instance, the industry had a record year.[7] Operating margins (income before taxes and interest) reached a five-year high with operating income at 19.5 percent and operating cash flow (income before taxes, interest, amortization, and depreciation) at 25.6 percent. Advertising accounts for about 80 percent of newspaper revenues. In 1997, advertising expenditures in newspapers increased 8.6 percent to $41.3 billion, and income from circulation was up 1 percent. Total spending on daily newspapers is expected to maintain a healthy annual growth rate, reaching $66 billion by 2002.[8]

The number of daily newspapers in the United States decreased gradually throughout the 1900's. The number peaked in 1909-10, when 2,202 newspapers were published.[9] After 1910, the

---

Review, September/October 1996: 11-12.

[7] Data about the newspaper industry are from the Newspaper Association of America's web site at *http://www.naa.org/info/facts99*.

[8] Veronis, Schuler & Associates, Inc., *Robust ad spending and circulation turnaround predicted for newspaper industry through 2002*, *http://www.veronissuhler.com/newspub/ segment.html*.

[9] Raymond B. Nixon, *Trends in U.S. Newspaper Ownership: Concentration with Competition*, Gazette 14 (1968): 181-193.

number began a gradual decline so that by 1946 there were 1,763 dailies.

Over the next 15 years, from 1946-1960, the number of daily newspapers remained stable. Beneath the surface of stability, however, significant change and restructuring occurred in the nature of competition. Historically, newspapers were located in major cities and faced competition from other newspapers published in the same city. In 1909-10, the 2,202 dailies were in 1,207 cities.[10] Of these cities, only 509 (42.2 percent of the cities that had a newspaper) had one newspaper. But by 1961, most newspapers faced no competition from other daily newspapers in their traditional urban market. Of the 1,461 cities with daily newspapers in 1961, 95.8 percent had no local daily newspaper competition. At the same time, between 1946 and 1960 Americans moved to the suburbs, and new daily newspapers sprang up in these towns and cities, which historically had no daily newspaper.

Newspapers in major cities also faced increased competition from television. Newspaper readers, who customarily bought two or more newspapers each day, found that television could supply them with late-breaking news. As a result of this increased competition, a number of newspapers in major metropolitan areas merged and some were closed.

By 1980, there were 1,745 dailies, a drop of only 18 newspapers since 1960. But since 1980, there has been a steady decline in the number of dailies. In the 1990's, the count went from 1,611 to 1,489.

A number of newspaper companies historically published two newspapers, morning and evening. In recent years, many of these companies closed their evening newspaper, while others combined their morning and evening newspapers into "all-day" newspapers. These "all-day" newspapers publish editions throughout the day, with each edition targeted at specific geographical audiences. Readers in suburban areas, who in the past could subscribe to a morning or an evening paper or both, now could only subscribe to the morning paper.

---

[10] Ibid.

Number of Newspapers, 1950-1998

Year	Morning	Evening	Total Daily Newspapers*	Sunday
1950	322	1450	1772	549
1955	316	1454	1760	541
1960	312	1459	1763	563
1965	320	1444	1751	562
1970	334	1429	1748	586
1975	339	1436	1756	639
1980	387	1388	1745	735
1985	482	1220	1676	798
1987	511	1166	1645	820
1988	529	1141	1642	840
1989	530	1125	1626	847
1990	559	1084	1611	863
1991	571	1042	1586	874
1992	596	995	1570	891
1993	623	954	1556	884
1994	656	891	1533	886
1995	656	891	1533	888
1996	686	846	1520	890
1997	705	816	1509	903
1998	721	781	1489	897

*All-day newspapers are listed in both morning and evening columns but only once in the total

While the number of daily newspapers has declined, the number of Sunday newspapers has increased significantly. In 1950, there were 549 Sunday newspapers; by 1998, there were 897, an increase of 63.3 percent.

Just as the number of newspapers has declined, so too has

newspaper circulation and readership.[11] Daily newspaper circulation peaked in 1987 with 62.8 million subscribers. Since then, it has steadily declined, dropping to 56.2 million subscribers in 1998, a loss of 10.5 percent. The decline is even steeper in view of the 23 percent growth in the adult population from 1980 to 1998. Circulation of Sunday newspapers has also declined from a high of 62.6 million in 1993 to 60.1 million in 1998. But this still represents a 26 percent gain in circulation since 1960.

---

[11] Circulation measures the number of daily newspapers purchased; readership measures the number of adults who read a daily newspaper.

Newspaper Circulation 1960-1998

Year	Total Daily Newspaper Circulation	Sunday Circulation
1960	58,881,746	47,698,651
1965	60,357,563	48,600,090
1970	62,107,527	49,216,602
1975	60,655,431	51,096,393
1980	62,201,840	54,671,755
1985	62,766,232	58,825,978
1986	62,502,036	58,924,518
1987	62,826,273	60,111,863
1988	62,694,816	61,747,189
1989	62,649,218	62,008,154
1990	62,324,156	62,634,512
1991	60,687,125	62,067,820
1992	60,164,499	62,159,971
1993	59,811,594	62,565,574
1994	59,305,436	62,294,799
1995	58,193,397	61,529,296
1996	56,989,808	60,797,814
1997	56,727,902	60,486,463
1998*	56,182,092	60,060,828

*Preliminary Data

Newspaper readership has also declined over the past three decades. In 1970, 77.6 percent of the adult population read a daily newspaper. By 1998, the percentage of adults reading a daily newspaper had dropped to 58.6 percent. The decline in readership for Sunday newspapers has not been as extreme, declining from 72.3 percent of adults in 1970 to 68.2 percent in 1998. Nevertheless, newspapers still reach more adults than do any other mass medium. Prime-time television reached only 40.8 percent of adults in 1998, a decline of 4.5 percent since 1996.

Readership, 1970-1998

Year	Weekday Readers % of Total Adult Population	Sunday/Weekend Readers % of Total Adult Population
1970	77.60%	72.3%
1977	68.50	67.9
1980	66.90	67.4
1982	67.00	66.6
1984	65.10	65.4
1985	64.20	65.1
1986	62.90	64.1
1987	64.80	65.7
1988	64.20	64.0
1989	63.60	67.0
1990	62.40	67.1
1991	62.10	66.9
1992	62.60	68.4
1993	61.70	69.0
1994	61.50	70.4
1995	64.20	72.6
1996	58.80	68.5
1997	58.70	68.5
1998	58.60	68.2

The demographics of newspaper readers show them to be upscale and older than non-readers. The typical newspaper reader is a college graduate, over the age of 35, earning more than $40,000, and a home-owner. In general, the better-educated and wealthier a person is, the greater likelihood that he or she will subscribe to a newspaper. Single-copy newspaper buyers share similar characteristics. These are exactly the type of readers advertisers want. [12]

---

[12] See Chapter V for further discussion of circulation.

Despite decreases in the number of subscribers and in readership, newspaper revenues have shown steady growth. The two primary sources of revenues for newspapers are circulation and advertising. Advertising represents by far the largest revenue source, accounting for about 70 to 80 percent of total revenues.

Newspaper Circulation and Advertising Revenues 1970-1998

Year	Total Circulation (000)	Total Advertising (000)	Total Revenues (000)	Percent Advertising
1970	$2,634,402	$5,704,000	$8,338,402	68.40%
1975	3,921,515	8,234,000	12,155,515	67.70
1980	5,469,589	14,794,000	20,263,589	73.00
1985	7,659,297	25,270,000	32,929,297	76.70
1990	8,500,000 (est.)	32,280,000	40,780,000	79.20
1995	9,720,186	36,092,000	45,812,186	78.80
1998	10,266,955	43,925,000	54,191,955	81.10

Circulation revenues, aided by higher prices, have shown small increases each year since 1985, with the exception of 1988.

Newspapers' advertising revenues, meanwhile, have shown dramatic gains. Expenditures for advertising in newspapers increased from $4.4 billion in 1965 to $43.9 billion in 1998, an increase of 892.4 percent. With the exceptions of the recession years of 1990-92, advertising expenditures have increased yearly by between 5 and 6 percent.

The three major categories of newspaper advertising are national, retail (local), and classified. Retail advertising has traditionally been the largest source of newspaper revenue. However, the percentage of revenue attributed to retail advertising has been slowly declining. In 1965, 54.9 percent of newspaper ad revenues came from retail advertising; by 1998, it accounted for 46.3 percent. The percentage of national advertising revenue also dropped during the same period, from 17.7 percent in 1965 to 13 percent in 1998. The largest growth in advertising revenue has been in classified advertising. In 1998 it accounted for 40.7 percent of newspaper advertising revenues, compared to 27.4 percent in 1965.

The almost uninterrupted climb in newspaper advertising revenues is matched by an almost equally uninterrupted descent in the share of ad dollars going to newspapers. In 1981, nearly 28 percent of total advertising expenditures were for newspaper ads; by 1999, newspapers' slice of the ad pie had dropped to just a shade over 22 percent. Moreover, classified advertising, an increasingly hefty proportion of the total newspaper ad take, is considered to be the source of newspaper ad revenue most vulnerable to online competition.

To protect their franchise, newspapers have established a strong presence on the Web. As of 1998, more than 750 dailies had on-line services, and 98 of the 100 largest papers had a Web site. Online classifieds are sold by more than 75 percent of the papers with Web sites.

Newspaper companies have done well financially, primarily because of their ability to attract advertising. They have done this, in the face of declining circulation, penetration, and readership, in part by stressing to advertisers the upscale character of their reader-customers. No wonder, then, that newspapers have been eager to zone editions to cultivate those readers in suburbia. Simultaneously, they have shown much less interest in less-affluent potential customers, even to the point of upping prices, knowing that they would discourage down-market readership.

B. An Overview of Publicly Traded Newspaper Companies

The publicly traded newspaper company segment of the industry comprises 17 companies whose core business is newspaper publishing. They are a major force in the industry. Thirteen of these companies are among the top 20 newspaper companies in circulation. Together, the 17 companies own 313 daily newspapers, which represented 21 percent of all dailies published in 1998. They also own 244 Sunday papers, 27.2 percent of the total of Sunday papers.

Their combined daily circulation of 24.7 million is 43.9 percent of total daily newspaper circulation. Their combined Sunday circulation is 30.9 million, 51.5 percent of total Sunday circulation. Of the 20 largest newspapers by circulation, 12 are owned by one of the 17 companies. The companies publish both highly respected newspapers and others that are not especially respected.

Total revenues of the companies exceeded $26 billion in 1998. In 1997, four of the companies had newspaper revenues of $2 billion or more.

Number of Newspapers Owned and Circulation
1998

Newspaper Company	Daily Circulation	Number of Dailies	Sunday Circulation	Number of Sunday Newspapers
Gannett	5,994,347	74	5,958,260	62
Knight Ridder	3,871,563	33	5,398,593	29
Times Mirror	2,370,848	9	3,559,285	7
Dow Jones	2,311,966	20	443,391	13
New York Times	2,252,610	20	3,142,254	16
E.W. Scripps	1,330,135	20	1,522,773	16
McClatchy	1,311,208	11	1,842,115	11
Tribune	1,264,417	4	1,859,573	4
A.H. Belo	895,538	7	1,284,190	7
Media General	820,937	22	947,889	18
Washington Post	813,036	2	1,143,150	3
Hollinger	802,554	27	656,008	11
Central	798,237	7	1,043,701	5
Lee Enterprises	622,598	21	721,740	16
Journal Register	532,472	18	511,966	13
Gray Commun.	107,000	3	39,000	1
Pulitzer	581,028	15	864,176	12
Total	**24,680,494**	**313**	**30,938,064**	**244**

The roots of nearly all of the companies can be traced to a founding individual. When the founder died, ownership transferred to family. Beginning in the late 1960s and continuing into the 1970s, the newspaper industry underwent consolidation as companies acquired additional newspapers. Inheritance taxes forced many families to sell their newspapers. Companies competed fiercely to buy the papers, often paying 10 or more times a newspaper's revenues.

Beginning in the 1960's, in order to generate capital to finance acquisitions, to reduce indebtedness, and to fend off hostile takeover attempts, newspaper companies went public. Prominent among these were Dow Jones, Gannett, Gray Communication, Lee Enterprises, Media General, New York Times, and Times Mirror. When some of the companies went public, the founding families attempted to maintain control of the company by issuing two or more classes of stock, with the family maintaining control through ownership of stock that gave them majority voting power.

A.H. Belo Corporation

The A.H. Belo Company dates to 1842 and went public in 1981. It owns six daily newspapers with a combined circulation of 910,000. It owns 17 television stations, reaching 14.3 percent of the U.S. television households, manages four television stations, and owns four local or regional cable news channels. Its newspaper segment accounts for 56 percent of the company's revenues.

Central Newspapers

The Central Newspapers Company was formed in 1934 by Eugene Pulliam and went public in 1989. The company owns seven daily newspapers with a total circulation of 832,000, an 80 percent share of the Westech group of companies, which organizes job fairs, publishes career magazines, and maintains a resume web site for the high tech industry, an 80 percent share in Home Buyer's Fair LLC, which provides Internet-based services and information for people who are moving and for corporations relocating employees. It also owns a direct marketing services company and a minority interest in a newsprint mill and a commercial printer.

Dow Jones & Company

The Dow Jones Company was founded in 1882 and went public in 1963. It owns the *Wall Street Journal*, the *Asian Wall Street Journal*, the *Wall Street Journal Europe* and the *Wall Street Journal Americas*, which have a total circulation of 4.1 million. The company also owns *Barron's* and 19 dailies with a total circulation of 568,000, and 15 weekly newspapers. The company owns Dow Jones Interactive Publishing, the Wall Street Journal Interactive Edition, and two radio services that produce business and financial reports for radio stations. The company also has a minority interest in a number of publishing and information companies in the United States and abroad.

E.W. Scripps Company

E.W. Scripps Company, one of the country's oldest newspaper companies, went public in 1998. It owns 19 daily newspapers with a total circulation of 1.3 million, nine network-affiliated television stations, Home & Garden Television, the Television Food Network, and a 12 percent interest in FOX SportSouth, a regional cable television network. The company syndicates and licenses news features and comics. The newspaper segment represents 59.5 percent of the company's revenues.

Gannett Company

The Gannett Company was founded in 1906 and went public in 1967. It owns *USA Today*, which has a circulation of 2.2 million, 74 dailies with a combined circulation of 6.7 million, and a variety of non-daily publications, including *USA Weekend*, a weekly magazine. The company also owns 21 television stations, a news service, and commercial printing companies. The newspaper segment accounts for 81.2 percent of the company's revenues; broadcasting accounts for 14.1 percent.

Gray Communications Systems

The Gray Communications Company went public in 1995. It owns three daily newspapers with a total circulation of 107,000, and one weekly shopper. The company owns 10 network-affiliated television stations, paging operations and a satellite uplink business. Broadcasting accounts for 70.6 percent of the company's revenues; publishing accounts for 22.8 percent.

Hollinger International
Hollinger International, which went public in 1994, is controlled by Hollinger, Inc. The Hollinger Company directly owns three daily newspapers in the United States, including the *Chicago Sun Times*. It also owns 78 non-daily newspapers and the Community Group, which consists of 166 newspapers and related publications. The company's 54 daily newspapers have a combined circulation of 1.1 million. Its 108 non-daily newspapers have a combined circulation of 1.5 million. Its 79 free publications have a circulation of 1.5 million. For accounting and management purposes, the *Jerusalem Post* is included in the Community Group.

The Journal Register Company
The Journal Register Company was formed in 1990 and completed its initial public offering in 1997. The company owns 24 daily newspapers and 185 non-daily publications.[13] Daily newspaper circulation is 652,000 and non-daily circulation is about 3.7 million. The company owns four commercial printing operations and a firm that develops software for the newspaper industry.

Knight Ridder, Inc.
Knight Ridder resulted from the 1974 merger of Knight Newspapers and Ridder Publications, each of which had been public companies since 1969. The Knight Ridder Company owns 31 daily newspapers with a combined circulation of 3.9 million, and 21 non-

---

[13] Journal Register has announced its intention to sell its Midwestern newspapers, leaving it with 20 dailies and 143 nondaily newspapers. The reason given for selling the papers is to lift the price of the company's stock. Lucia Moses, *Journal Register Sheds Papers in wake of Thomson sell-off*, Editor & Publisher, March 6, 2000, p. 14.

daily newspapers with a combined circulation of 9.2 million. It is also a partner in two newsprint mills.

Lee Enterprises

Lee Enterprises was founded in 1890 and went public in 1969. The company owns 21 daily newspapers with a circulation of 623,000. It owns 11 weekly newspapers with a combined circulation of 66,800, 41 shoppers with a non-paid circulation of 1.7 million, and other specialty publications. The company owns nine television stations.[14] Its publishing segment accounts for 74 percent of the company's revenues.

The McClatchy Company

The McClatchy Company dates to the California Gold Rush era of 1857, when James McClatchy founded the *Sacramento Bee*. It went public in 1988. The company owns 11 daily newspapers with a combined circulation of 1.4 million. It also owns 12 non-daily newspapers with an average circulation of 65,000. In addition, it owns an online publishing company and is a part owner of a newsprint mill.

Media General, Inc.

The Media General Company was founded in 1879 and went public as Richmond Newspapers, Inc., in 1966. Richmond Newspapers, Inc., created Media General as a holding company in 1969. The company owns 21 daily and nearly 100 weekly newspapers and periodicals. Daily newspaper circulation is approximately 840,000. Media General owns a 40 percent stake in the *Denver Post*, which has a circulation of 337,000. The company owns 14 network-affiliated television stations, two cable systems, a cable advertising firm, and an interest in a cable advertising interconnect business serving five cable systems in the Washington,

---

[14] The company announced in March 2000 that it intends to sell its broadcasting segment in order to focus on its core publishing and on-line business, *Lee: Bye-bye, Broadcast!*, Editor & Publisher, March 6, 2000, pp. 3-4.

D.C., area. It also owns a newsprint mill and has part interest in a second mill. Its publishing segment accounts for 53 percent of revenues, broadcasting for 18 percent.

The New York Times Company
　　The New York Times Company went public in 1967. It owns 20 newspapers, including the *New York Times* and the *Boston Globe*, with a total daily circulation of 2.3 million and a Sunday circulation of 3.2 million. The company owns eight television and two radio stations, golfing magazines, a part interest in forest-product ventures, and has a 50 percent interest in the *International Herald Tribune*. The newspaper-publishing segment accounts for 91 percent of total revenues.

The Pulitzer Publishing Company
　　The Pulitzer Company was founded in 1878 by Joseph Pulitzer, and went public in 1986 after a hostile takeover attempted by members of the Pulitzer family. It owns 14 newspapers with a total circulation of 581,000. Two of its newspapers, *The* (Tucson) *Star* and the *St. Louis Post-Dispatch*, account for 72.5 percent of company circulation. The remaining 12 newspapers have a combined circulation of 159,000. In 1998, the company spun off its nine network-affiliated television stations and five radio stations to Hearst-Argyle. The company also has an interest in the Arizona Diamondbacks and St. Louis Cardinals baseball teams.

The Tribune Company
　　The Tribune Company was founded in 1847, and went public in 1983. It owns four newspapers, the most prominent of which is *The Chicago Tribune*, with a combined daily circulation of 1.3 million and a Sunday circulation of 1.9 million. The publishing segment generated about 50 percent of the company's operating revenues in 1998. The company owns 19 television and four radio stations. It is involved in syndication, advertising-placement services, cable-television programming, and Internet and online-related business activities. The company owns the Chicago Cubs baseball team and an entertainment company that develops and distributes

television programming. Its education segment publishes books and other educational materials.

The Times Mirror Company

Prior to its takeover by the Tribune, the Times Mirror Company had been restructuring, recapitalizing, and overhauling its operations. The company owned seven English-language dailies and had a 50 percent interest in a Spanish-language daily published in Southern California. Total daily circulation was 2.4 million, Sunday circulation 3.1 million. In 1998, the company acquired 24 shoppers in Southern California. The company owned a number of specialty consumer magazines. The company's stock started trading on the New York Stock Exchange in 1964.

The Washington Post Company

The Washington Post Company went public in 1971. It owns two daily newspapers with a combined daily circulation of 830,000, the *Washington Post National Weekly Edition* with a circulation of 92,000, and the Gazette Newspapers, which publish one paid-circulation and 30 controlled-circulation weekly community newspapers with a total circulation of 443,000, and 50 percent of the *International Herald Tribune.* The company owns six network-affiliated television stations and 53 cable television systems. The company publishes *Newsweek* and its several spin-off publications. The Post-Newsweek Business Information, Inc., subsidiary publishes trade periodicals and produces trade shows for the information-technology industry. The company owns Kaplan Educational Centers, Inc., which prepares students to take standardized tests; Washingtonpost.Newsweek Interactive Company, which develops news and information products for electronic distribution; and Legi-Slate, Inc., a computerized database containing information on legislative and regulatory activities of the U.S. government.

C. Financial Performance

As a group, the 17 publicly traded newspaper companies are highly profitable. In 1998, operating profit margins (revenues minus expenses before interest and taxes) averaged 18.7 percent, ranging from 7.1 percent (Times Mirror) to 28.2 percent (Gannett). Net income (after interest, depreciation and taxes) for most of the companies increased at a healthy rate over the past decade. The companies have served investors well. For 10 of the 17 companies, return on shareholder investment between 1994-97 was greater than that of the S&P 500. For half (eight) of the companies, shareholder return exceeded that of their peer group between 1994-97. Between 1992 and 1997, stock prices of seven of the 16 companies more than doubled. Central Newspapers had the largest increase, with its stock increasing in value by 223.2 percent.

Financial Performance 1998
(000)

Company	Circulation Revenues	Advertising Revenues	Total Revenues (all business segments)	Operating Income**	Net Income*	Profit Margins
McClatchy	$162,433	$756,052	$968,651	$180,858	$61,051	18.6%
A.H. Belo	94,500	669,000	1,407,34	233,085	64,902	16.6
Knight Ridder	587,529	2,362,859	3,091,919	504,618	365,857	22.8
Gannett	1,010,238	2,942,995	5,121,291	1,443,502	999,913	28.2
Hollinger International	131,983	416,831	2,197,760	282,079	196,912	12.8
Gray Communication	5,315	23,265	128,890	24,927	403,000	19.3
Washington Post	N/A***	NA***	2,110,360	378,897	417,259	18.0
Dow Jones	465,455	1,031,210	2,158,106	218,573	8,362	10.1
Central Newspapers	150,446	562,408	752,690	153,952	89,351	20.5
E.W. Scripps	152,829	647,492	1,455,000	276,000	131,214	19.0
Journal Register	89,388	312,908	426,780	119,067	41,139	27.9
Lee Enterprises	81,912	195,852	517,293	112,847	62,233	21.8
Media General	N/A	N/A	973,978	156,030	70,874	16.0
New York Times	678,784	2,073,540	2,936,705	515,220	278,914	17.5
Times Mirror	434,400	1,787,300	3,000,085	212,563	1,417,338	7.1
Tribune Co.	243,842	1,161,939	2,980,899	702,289	414,272	23.6
Pulitzer	N/A***	N/A***	372,924	42,921	76,284	20.4
Total	4,289,054	14,943,651	30,227,752	5,514,507	5,022,591	18.7

*Net income is income after taxes and interest.
**Operating income is income before taxes and interest.
***Information not reported.

Percentage Increase in Stock Price, 1992-1997

Company	% increase in per-share price 1992-97
Central Newspapers	223.20%
Pulitzer	188.20
Times Mirror	173.30
New York Times	150.70
Gannett	143.50
Media General	140.60
Dow Jones	98.90
Knight Ridder	72.70
McClatchy*	43.90
A. H. Belo	33.60
E.W. Scripps**	23.00
Tribune Co.	21.00
Lee Enterprises	-11.30
Washington Post	144.2****
Gray Communications	268.4****
Hollinger International	3.7****

*1993-97

**1995-97

***Journal Register is not included because it became a public company in 1997

****The company did not report the percentage increase in its share price between 1992-97. The percentage increase was calculated by the difference in the price of the stock at the close of trading on January 1, 1992 and the close of trading on December 31, 1997.

Stock Market Return on Shareholder Investment, 1992-1997

Company	Shareholder Return	S&P 500	Peer Group
Pulitzer	257%	179%	152%
Central Newspapers	243	158	141
E.W. Scripps	238	152	157
Gray Communication	229	129	76
Times Mirror	219	152	167
A.H. Belo*	183	151	161
Tribune Co.	182	151	162
New York Times	176	151	165
Gannett	172	152	175
Media General***	160	72	179
Washington Post	129	152	179
Dow Jones	125	152	126
Knight Ridder	101	152	162
Lee Enterprises	99	157	148
McClatchy**	92	127	150
Hollinger International****	12	108	90

*NYSE Market Index
**S&P MidCap 400 Index
***AMEX Composite Index
****Years 1994-1997
Differences in S&P percentage reflect differences in the date of reporting at fiscal-year end for some companies

Earnings before interest, taxes, depreciation and amortization (EBITDA) are widely used by analysts and investors to evaluate the performance of media companies. Not all companies report EBITDA and those that do will not necessarily calculate it using the same methods. Nevertheless, EBITDA is a standard measure of performance in the media industry. Some companies report operating cash flow instead of EBITDA. Operating cash flow is defined as earnings from operations plus depreciation and amortization. Operating cash flow is a measure of financial performance used to compare media companies.

Thirteen companies report either EBITDA or operating cash flow. As a percentage of revenue, EBITDA or operating cash flow ranges from a high of 34.4 percent for Journal Register to a low of 10.6 percent for the Washington Post. The average EBITDA or operating cash flow as a percent of revenue is 27 percent for the companies that report these data–data which show that newspapers do generate large cash flows, allowing companies to finance acquisitions of other newspapers.

EBITDA
(Millions)

COMPANY	EBITDA	REVENUES	EBITDA AS PERCENT OF REVENUES
Journal Register	$146.7	$426.8	34.4
Dow Jones	437.1	2,158.1	20.2
Tribune	898.0	2,980.9	30.1
Lee Enterprises	150.5	517.3	29.1
E.W. Scripps	380.0	1,455.0	26.1
Central Newspapers	199.4	752.7	26.5
New York Times	725.0	2,937.7	24.7
Hollinger	109.2	589.2	18.5
Gray Comm*	46.6	128.9	36.2
Washington Post*	223.1	2,110.4	10.6
Gannett*	1,753.7	5,121.3	34.2
A.H. Belo*	442.2	1,407.3	31.4
Media General	284.5	974.0	29.1

* Operating Cash Flow instead of EBITDA

Examining the financial performance of the companies over the past three years shows that the newspaper companies have seen significant growth in income and cash flow, often exceeding revenue growth. For eight of the 15 companies, net income increased faster than revenues. For 12 of 16 companies, operating income grew at a greater percentage than did revenues. And for 10 of the 12 companies, EBITDA or operating cash flow increased at a higher rate than did revenues. These data indicate that publicly traded newspaper companies have seen significant growth in their cash flow, despite modest growth in revenues. This can only be accounted for by increased efficiency and reduction of expenses.

FINANCIAL PERFORMANCE
Percent Change 1996-1998

Company	Revenue	Net Income	Operating Income	EBITDA
Hollinger	3.00	N/A	8.90	2.30
New York Times	11.80	229.90	197.70	42.70
Central Newspapers	21.30	37.80	46.00	41.40
Knight Ridder	30.30	36.60	51.50	N/A
E.W. Scripps	36.60	0.70	34.00	106.50
Lee Enterprises	21.00	36.90	51.50	N/A
Times Mirror	8.40	586.50**	-26.90	N/A
McClatchy	55.20	50.00	123.10	N/A
Tribune	23.90	11.30	39.50	39.00
Dow Jones	-13.00	-95.60	-35.10	-21.20
Journal Register	42.40	98.60	48.90	48.80
A.H. Belo*	70.70	-25.80	76.30	40.70
Gannett*	15.80	6.00	35.40	29.50
Washington Post	13.90	89.00	-85.50	-21.90
Media General*	27.30	0.53	52.30	46.80
Gray Commun.*	62.50	178.10	297.10	66.80

*Operating cash flow instead of EBITDA.
**There was a substantial after-tax gain related to discontinued operations.

Newspaper companies have been able to post these impressive numbers, and to lure investors who have multiple other investment choices, even in the face of declining circulation, readership, and advertising share. The chapters that follow will show how the feat has affected the content and marketing of newspapers and the way journalists work.

In the words of Michael R. Fancher, executive editor of the *Seattle Times*, "[Editors] wrestle with financial imperatives and marketing pressures. Many of us come into journalism because of our love of words and hatred of numbers, but the balance in our work has shifted. Our careers have evolved and we've taken a place at the table with advertising and circulation directors. We are held increasingly accountable for measurable results."[15]

Or as Sandra M. Rowe, editor of *The Oregonian* of Portland and former president of the American Society of Newspaper Editors, expressed it: "As editors have been pulled away from journalism by the demands of the admittedly increasingly competitive marketplace, they have put less of their passion into the journalism."[16]

---

[15] *"Extending the Brand,"* American Society of Newspaper Editors, p. 6.

[16] Video produced by Gannett Co. for American Society of Newspaper Editors.

Chapter III

Ownership and Control

It's commonplace, but accurate, to observe that while newspapers are a business, they are a different kind of business, one with an important societal role, with certain constitutional protections, and so on. When newspaper companies went public, they declared in effect that they wanted to be treated in the marketplace the same as any other business. And they are. In consequence, they become subject to external and internal forces that oblige them to behave as do other businesses, but with special consequences for journalism.

In this chapter, we examine some of those forces: boards of directors and their compensation policies, investors in the companies, stock analysts who follow the companies and who advise the investors, the CEO's who deal with analysts and investors and who run the companies. A common theme is the central role of profits and stock price in the publicly traded newspaper company, and how that plays out in the newsroom.

A. Boards of Directors

The Oregonian editor Sandra Rowe has lauded Tom Johnson, former president and publisher of the *Los Angeles Times*, for urging that top executives of media companies have news experience and news values prominent in their portfolios. "Who better to lead these organizations," she quoted Johnson, "than those who have the core values of journalism?"[17]

---

[17] *"Amid the Constant Criticism Some See A Future For Us,"* American Editor, p. 2 (June 1997).

Rowe and Johnson could have made the same point about the boards of directors of newspaper companies. Directors are in key positions to influence the quality of a company's publications by how much attention they pay to journalistic objectives, and by the incentives they establish to achieve them.

The boards of newspaper companies, however, resemble other corporate boards in that they draw heavily from industry, finance and law for outside (non-employee) directors. Of the 131 outside directors on the boards of the 17 companies, only 17 (13 percent) have had experience on the editorial side of a news organization. Seven companies have no outside directors with a newspaper background; a half-dozen have just one. By contrast, four of McClatchy's nine outside directors have worked as journalists. They account for nearly a fourth of all outside directors in the 17 companies who have backgrounds in journalism. In addition, an editor, McClatchy's vice president for news, is a director.

According to McClatchy CEO Gary B. Pruitt, journalism issues occupy the board. The company has a Newspaper Review Committee, which includes two board members in addition to several former editors, who periodically review 2½ weeks of each of the company's papers. The board approves budgets for each company paper, including newshole, the number of full-time employees or their equivalent (FTEs), and news budgets. The board meets once a year at a newspaper site, where it visits with community members and newspaper staff. Editors of the papers attend board meetings on a rotating basis. A distinguished retired Knight Ridder editor, Larry Jinks, is a director and he serves on the board's compensation committee.

Does the presence on the board of a number of former journalists explain the attention McClatchy's board gives to journalism issues? Jinks believes it's the other way around. He attributes his own appointment to the board, and both his membership on the compensation committee, and its policies, to an existing commitment by McClatchy to journalism. Whether the chicken or egg comes first, directors who have journalism backgrounds surely can reinforce a corporate culture that values journalistic achievement.

B. Ownership Structure

Two general types of ownership can be identified among the 17 publicly traded newspaper companies. The first, and less typical, are companies that have a single class of common stock, all of which is traded publicly. Gannett and Knight Ridder best represent this form of ownership.[18] More typical are companies with two or more classes of stock, with ownership of certain classes limited to founding family and their descendants. In most cases, the family-owned stock has voting power of 10 to 1 over the stock traded publicly.

In the cases of McClatchy, E.W. Scripps, Media General and the New York Times, further restrictions are placed on the number of directors elected by holders of the publicly traded stock, thus reserving control of the board to a founding or controlling group of owners. Family members and trustees of family trusts hold majority voting power in McClatchy, A. H. Belo, Hollinger International, Gray Communications, Washington Post, Central Newspapers, E.W. Scripps, Media General, New York Times, and Dow Jones. That was true also of Times Mirror.

---

[18] The Journal Register also has one class of stock, but 50 percent of it is owned by Warburg, Pincus, an investment firm.

Classes of Stock and Voting Rights of Publicly Traded Newspaper Companies

Company	Publicly Traded Stock	Voting Rights	Restricted Stock	Voting Rights
McClatchy	Class A	1/10 vote/sh	Class B	1 vote/sh elect 9 directors
Knight Ridder	Common	1 vote/sh	None	
A.H. Belo	Series A	1 vote/sh	Series B	10 votes/sh
Gannett	Common	1 vote/sh	None	
Hollinger International	Class A	1 vote/sh	Class B	10 votes/sh
Gray Communication	Class B	1 vote/sh	Class A	10 votes/sh
Washington Post	Class B	1 vote/sh	Class A	1 vote/sh
Dow Jones	Common	1 vote/sh	Class B	10 votes/sh
Central Newspapers	Class A	1/10 vote/sh	Class B	1 vote/sh
E.W. Scripps	Class A	1 vote/sh Elect 1/3 of board Restricted on voting on other issues	Common	1 vote/sh Elect 2/3 of board
Journal Register	Common	1 vote/sh	None	
Lee Enterprises	Common	1 vote/sh	Class B	10 votes/sh
Media General	Class A	1 vote/sh Elects 30% of board	Class B	1 vote/sh Elects 70% of board
New York Times	Class A	1 vote/sh Elects 5 of 15 board members	Class B	1 vote/sh Elects 10 of 15 board members
Tribune Company	Common	1 vote/sh	Preferred	9.16 votes/sh
Times Mirror	Series A	1 vote/sh	Series C	10 votes/sh
Pulitzer	Common	1 vote/sh	Class B	10 votes/sh

Whether membership in a particular family is good or bad for journalism depends, of course, on the individuals. Some descendants may have inherited a sense of public service along with their stock while others may see their stock in the company simply as another investment, and board membership as a way to maximize the family's returns.

While families may be in controlling positions by virtue of ownership of particular classes of stock, what matters in the marketplace is the publicly traded stock. The price of that stock is an ever-present concern of newspaper companies and, of course, their investors. The financial performance of the 17 companies has been strong, and record-setting in a number of cases in the past few years. Operating margins are high, advertising revenues are growing at a healthy pace, costs are controlled, and net income often is growing.

Prices of the publicly traded stock of these companies increased significantly over the past decade, frequently exceeding the S&P 500. It is not surprising, then, that institutional investors–among them banks, mutual funds, and pension funds–have been attracted to the companies. In 1999, institutions owned 66.69 percent of the stock with a total value of $43.5 billion. For 14 of the 17 companies, institutional investors owned a majority of the publicly traded stock.

The largest institutional investor in these companies is Barclays Bank. It is one of the 10 largest institutional investors in 14 of the 17 companies. In six of the companies, Goldman, Sachs and Bankers Trust are among the 10 largest institutional investors. State Street Corporation and J.P. Morgan are among the 10 largest institutional investors in four of the companies. Wellington Management is one of the 10 largest institutional investors in three of the companies.

An examination of ownership changes over a recent nine-month period showed significant variation in the ten largest institutional owners in a number of the companies. The liquidity of the stock market, and the willingness of big investors to shift holdings, gives big investors clout even without ownership of controlling classes of stock.

Thus, there's a division of power in newspaper companies with a strong family presence; families exercise it in the board room, institutional investors on the trading floor. Of the 11 newspaper companies in which family trusts dominate the boards, in only two, Gray and E.W. Scripps, do institutional investors own less than a majority of the publicly traded shares, and the institutional ownership of Scripps is barely under 50 percent.

So even if a board is controlled by the most altruistic of family members, the reality is that directors and management must be attentive to the interests of institutional investors lest they dump their publicly traded stock and eviscerate the stock price.[19]

---

[19] For a detailed breakdown of institutional stock ownership for each company, see Appendix A.

III / Ownership and Control / 47

Institutional Ownership of Publicly Traded Stock, 1999

Company	% owned by institutional investors	% owned by 10 largest institutional investors	% owned by 5 largest institutional investors	% owned by largest institutional investor	Value of stock owned by institutional investors	Total market value of company's stock	Price per share	Number of Shares Owned by Institutions
Knight Ridder	84.77%	37.26%	26.16%	8.58%	$3,533,141,709	$4,167,915,193	$52.87	66,826,966
Pulitzer	35.68	24.91	17.45	6.63	205,755,997	576,670,395	81.19	2,534,253
Dow Jones	74.49	41.22	29.61	9.56	2,759,817,637	3,704,950,513	52.50	52,567,955
Gannett	79.50	22.11	14.24	3.62	16,046,212,530	20,183,915,132	72.25	222,092,907
A.H. Belo	69.19	30.93	21.12	6.82	1,512,983,908	2,186,708,929	22.06	68,584,946
New York Times	62.08	18.85	11.40	3.02	3,789,765,592	6,104,648,183	34.12	111,071,676
McClatchy	81.12	42.63	29.97	8.20	481,577,149	593,660,194	36.81	13,082,780
Media General	64.82	34.51	26.60	12.58	880,777,119	1,358,804,565	51.62	17,062,711
Lee Enterprises	68.26	36.64	28.81	10.95	648,797,715	950,480,098	29.00	22,372,335
Times Mirror	61.70	29.95	21.26	7.63	1,727,982,903	2,800,620,588	58.94	29,317,660
Washington Post	65.73	41.03	34.55	20.66	3,058,399,900	4,652,974,137	556.50	5,495,777
Tribune Co.	59.89	18.81	11.86	3.48	5,646,754,671	9,428,543,448	78.94	71,532,236
Central Newspapers	66.52	33.45	23.16	9.16	871,172,995	1,309,640,702	35.00	24,890,657
E.W. Scripps	48.63	22.50	13.80	3.87	1,355,615,610	2,787,611,783	47.12	28,769,431
Hollinger International	62.57	26.27	15.64	3.82	820,818,928	1,311,841,023	13.87	59,179,447
Gray Communications	20.54	15.14	11.44	4.22	22,196,290	108,063,729	15.81	1,403,940
Journal Register	21.04	13.66	9.78	2.75	172,942,444	821,969,791	17.37	9,956,387
					$43,534,713,097	$63,049,018,402		806,742,065
					69.05%			100.00%

In keeping an eye out for the interests of investors, board members also serve their own interests for, in almost every instance, the compensation of non-employee directors includes stock options or grants of stock or both. Only directors of Gannett and Washington Post receive strictly cash compensation for board service.[20]

A major responsibility of newspaper company boards of directors is to establish, through their compensation committees, financial incentives for management. Although stockholders at times must approve the broad outlines of company compensation plans, the details of who gets what annually either are set by the committees or are recommended by them to the board for approval. Either way, compensation committees are influential in determining how company managers are evaluated and the basis for their rewards. Money talks, so the way committees allocate it speaks eloquently about a company's values and objectives.

Of the 68 compensation committee members in the 17 companies we studied, all but three were outside directors. As noted, the boards of directors of newspaper companies resemble the boards of other publicly traded firms in that outside directors are drawn principally from the business world. The compensation committees likewise are heavily weighted with executives who have backgrounds in business.

Only six of the 68 committee members had experience in the kind of general-interest newspaper journalism in which the companies principally are engaged. The committees range in size from three to six members, with a membership average of four. No compensation committee has more than a single member who has relevant background as a working journalist; in 11 of the 17 companies, no one on the committee charged with making decisions that affect newsrooms has ever worked in one.

Compensation committees determine or recommend corporate salaries, bonuses, and stock-based awards. Salaries and bonuses usually are paid in cash, but executives at times receive a portion of

---

[20] For a picture of director compensation by company, see Appendix A.

their bonus in company stock. On salaries, the committees customarily rely on consultants, who use salary surveys (usually but not always of newspaper companies) and strive for base salaries for company officers at the median of comparable companies. Raises often are tied to "company performance," which customarily is measured by financial results such as operating income, earnings per share and growth in revenues, operating cash flow, and net income.

While annual reports to stockholders of publicly traded newspaper companies frequently extol quality in their publications and programs, seldom do compensation committee reports link salary increases to improvements in circulation or to quality of the company's output. McClatchy is an especially notable exception. Its committee report says salary and other components of the company's compensation package reward individual achievement as well as company performance. The latter is measured both by financial results and "growth in circulation, product excellence and market acceptance, sound strategic planning, development of new products and services, and community involvement and good corporate citizenship."

By and large, so little attention is paid to a company"s brand of journalism that it is possible to study a committee report of how top managers are rewarded and not realize that the enterprise discussed is engaged in journalism.

Bonuses account for a hefty portion of the cash compensation of newspaper company managers. In some companies, they are equal to half or more of salaries and sometimes dwarf them. The common thread in bonus awards is their heavy dependence on bottom-line performance, as determined by a variety of financial yardsticks, including earnings per share, operating cash flow, and operating profit.

While many of the firms tie bonuses exclusively to meeting corporate financial targets, some reserve a small portion of the bonus to how well executives achieve individual pre-established goals. (At Knight Ridder, 35 percent of bonuses were tailored to individual objectives, 65 percent to "the financial performance of the company compared to budget.")

Compensation committee reports seldom specify what individual managers must do to earn their awards. When they are specific, they rarely include mention of journalistic performance. Exceptions include a reference to "editorial enhancements" at the *New York Times*, credited to the company's chairman and CEO, and acknowledgment of "continued improvement in the quality of news content," in the case of McClatchy's vice president for news.

The attention Gannett gives to journalistic quality in its pay decisions is somewhat ambiguous. At one point in its report, Gannett's compensation committee noted that it emphasizes "the important link between the compensation of its executive officers and the company's performance relative to its business objectives." The company's business objectives are "increasing shareholder value, performance against budget, product quality and employee development." However, the committee said that compensation decisions are based on "earnings per share, operating income as a percentage of sales, return on assets, return on equity, operating cash flow, stock price and market value." It's unclear, therefore, whether or how much considerations of journalistic quality figure in compensation awards.

As a general proposition, it's safe to say that when it comes to bonuses, the overwhelming emphasis by newspaper companies is on rewards for financial rather than journalistic performance. The message from compensation committees to most publicly traded newspaper company managers, therefore, is unmistakable: Your take-home pay, in salary and bonuses, depends in substantial part on making the newspaper business as profitable as possible.

The third leg of the compensation stool is company stock, which is used both as a retention device and as incentive. Gannett's committee reasons: "Executive officers should benefit together with shareholders as the company's stock increases in value. Stock awards successfully focus executives' attention on managing the company from the perspective of an owner with an equity stake in the business." Modest variations on this theme appear repeatedly in compensation committee reports.

The two most common forms of stock awards are restricted stock and stock options. Restricted stock is awarded with conditions, such as a prohibition on transferring shares or forfeiture of shares for leaving the company. The restrictions, which may lapse after several years, are intended to help bind recipients to the company.

Stock options have value only if the stock appreciates. Options are awarded at a fixed price, customarily the market price at time of the award, and that price typically remains frozen until the recipient exercises the option. Options usually are staggered so that they are exercisable during three- or four-year periods over a 10-year span. It's not uncommon for key executives to be awarded tens of thousands of stock options that can be worth millions in a rising market.

While mainly used as a device to align the interests of top executives with shareholders, stock options also find their way into the compensation packages of lower-level employees. At the New York Times Co., in addition to all executive officers and employee directors, approximately 490 other employees are eligible for options grants. Stock options have become a way also to incentivize key newsroom employees. In our interviews with editors[21] we found that fully three-fourths were awarded stock options.

Because stock options are intended to pay off over time, they frequently are included in the long-term compensation plans of newspaper companies. In theory, that should encourage stock-option recipients to look beyond short-term quarterly results. Cash compensation, however, tied as it often is to financial performance in the recent past, tugs in the opposite direction. In any event, executives have to be mindful that, if they preside over a quarter that falls short of Wall Street expectations, the price of their company's stock (and their own) can be devastated.

As with salary and bonuses, stock-option awards depend heavily on financial yardsticks. Dow Jones, for instance, ties stock awards to "total stockholder return, return on equity, earnings growth, profit margins, and other financial criteria." Unlike most other compensation committees, however, the Dow Jones committee cites also "quality of Dow Jones' publications and services, development of products and services for a global marketplace, quality of customer

---

[21] See Chapter IV, *infra*.

service and level of customer satisfaction, development of human resources, including the recruitment and advancement of women and minorities."

Internal Revenue Code Section 162 (m) provides that annual compensation in excess of $1 million paid to a public company's five highest-paid executives is deductible for the company only if it is based on "objective performance goals." A performance goal is objective "if a third person having knowledge of the relevant facts could determine whether the goal is met." To be deductible, the compensation plans and criteria must be approved by stockholders.

The criteria overwhelmingly favored by compensation committees are financial–earnings per share, operating income and the like–in part because financial measures are easier to apply and doubtless also because increasing shareholder value is an overriding objective. There appears to be no reason that quality-related goals, such as non-advertorial newshole, circulation,[22] extent of enterprise journalism, and recognition by peers, could not qualify as "objective performance goals" and be the basis for incentive compensation. In other words, if compensation committees prefer to reward strictly financial performance, it is not because Uncle Sam makes them do it. In any case, if stock options and other incentive-pay awards linked to achieving a particular quality goal might be held not deductible, a company could always opt to forgo deductibility.

C. Investment-oriented Management

Since stock options are valuable only to the extent that a company's stock price increases, and awards are influenced by financial factors, it's scarcely surprising that the interest of shareholders in higher stock prices becomes also a preoccupation of management. When combined with the stress placed on the bottom line in making salary and bonus awards, it's little wonder that 90 percent of the editors we interviewed said they experienced pressure

---

[22] For discussion of the correlation between circulation and quality, see Chapter IV.

for higher profits. In a labor-intensive business, the pressure often is greatest on staffing. As will be observed in Chapter IV, a principal complaint of the editors concerned belt-tightening on payroll, the "chipping away at staff."

How news organizations have dealt with a relatively small corner of the news operation, pagination, provides an instructive insight into the way a focus on profit can take its toll in the newsroom.

A decade or two ago, it was the norm for newspaper pages to be prepared for reproduction and printing by composing-room personnel; they performed the mechanical task of pasting together the stories and other elements that made up each page, in accordance with layouts prepared in the newsroom. Nowadays, page makeup commonly is a newsroom function, done electronically on video display terminals. The shift from composing room to newsroom led to fewer composing-room employees, and to a heavier workload for the newsroom.

By most accounts, pagination has a number of pluses and is widely considered to be a superior way to produce newspaper pages. The extra burden on newsrooms is a major drawback. A study of pagination at a dozen papers by John Russial of the University of Oregon in the late 1980's found that it took newsroom personnel on average about 15 minutes more per page to paginate than to perform the tasks related to production they had done previously.[23] Russial commented: "As systems improve, pagination may take less time, but it is unlikely that the makeup burden that has shifted from the back shop to the newsroom will ever be erased by technological improvements"

"The burden," noted Russial, "is not trivial." He calculated that at a medium-size paper that paginates 50 pages a day, the extra work amounts to more than a shift a day; at a large paper, with 200 pages, it would be the equivalent of five shifts of staff time daily.

---

[23] John T. Russial, *Pagination and the Newsroom: A Question of Time*, Newspaper Research Journal, V.15, No. 1, P. 91 (Winter 1994).

Pagination at most papers is done by copy editors. Prior to the advent of pagination, their major responsibility had been to write headlines and to ride herd on copy for clarity and for grammatical, spelling, and factual mistakes. Traditionally, they were the last line of defense against newspaper error. Unless additional copy editors are hired to compensate for pagination, "quality is almost sure to suffer." Russial's decade-old warning was echoed recently by Melissa McCoy, foreign-desk copy chief for the *Los Angeles Times*:

"[Y]ou'd be hard-pressed to find a copy chief who doesn't marvel at the fact that more errors don't get into the newspaper considering increased production workloads, earlier deadlines and staff cutbacks. . . . If your paper relies heavily on pagination and production, add support staff to help with the computer work or risk losing a copy/news editor's time to coding. By using pagination, we may cut composing staff, but the work must be shifted somewhere, to someone. If it's shifting entirely to the [copy] desk, the final product is going to suffer."[24]

To Michael R. Fancher, executive editor of the *Seattle Times*, "the amount of production work that the copy desks have taken on is almost criminal."

We interviewed copy editors at 50 papers of diverse size and location owned by 15 publicly traded newspaper companies. Forty-six of the papers had been paginating from six months to 17 years. At nearly 70 percent of the paginating papers, 32 of the 46, pagination had been made an exclusive responsibility of copy editors. At the other 14 papers, split desks were established, one to edit copy, the other to paginate.

Only 11 of the 46 papers–a bit more than 20 percent–had increased staff to handle the extra work, with most of the increase occurring at papers with split desks. In some cases where staff had been added, editors said the increase was insufficient for the workload. Thirty-three of the papers–some 70 percent–had no increase in staff. Respondents at two papers were unsure. At the 32 papers where copy editors were both paginating and editing copy,

---

[24] *Http://www.Copydesk.org/credibility.htm* (dated 10/25/99).

they did it all: checked for errors, wrote headlines and cutlines, pulled stories from the wires, cropped and toned photos, placed all of it on their VDTs and, at times, prepared material for Web sites.

About 70 percent of the copy editors said that, since pagination, there was less time to devote to editing copy. A copy editor at a paper with 240,000 circulation estimated the time taken from copy editing chores at 40 percent while at another paper, circulation 80,000, it was estimated to be 10 percent. Copy editors were divided about whether this translated to greater inaccuracy. More than a third, 17, believed accuracy had declined while just more than half, 24, felt it was the same or not a factor. Many of the latter were among the 14 split-desk papers where copy editors did not have to both edit copy and paginate, and where staff had increased.

Errors are more or less measurable. Much more difficult to quantify are clarity and readability. It stands to reason that the push to move production from the composing room to the newsroom, without commensurate increases in newsroom staff, adversely affects quality.

A number of the CEOs we interviewed, when discussing staff, stressed that more is not necessarily better. The veteran former editor, Gene Roberts, observed that, while he has heard of papers with reduced staff that improved, he's never seen one. That observation seems to be particularly pertinent to pagination.[25] Piling on more work without adding staff, as has occurred repeatedly, is the equivalent of a cutback. It improves the bottom line at the expense of negative consequences for journalism. The editor who complained, "There's a direct line between Wall Street and the newsroom," could have had pagination in mind.

---

[25] Editor & Publisher, Dec. 28, 1996.

D. The Influence of the Investment Community: Analysts

The very large position of institutional investors in newspaper companies compels the companies to be accessible both to institutional investors and to stock analysts. To facilitate that, three formal meetings are held over several days each year at which key newspaper company executives address large numbers of analysts and investors.[26] Executives at the sessions describe their operating philosophies and performance, and they field questions. Some managers utilize the gatherings to huddle privately with major investors. Analysts and investors alike have ready access throughout the year to CEOs, CFOs, and stockholder-relations executives, by phone and by on-site visits.

An analyst told us: "I can get a meeting with senior management of Tribune any time I want. How many can do that?" Doors open readily for analysts, because they have the ears of institutional investors, which include heavy hitters whose marketplace clout can move stock prices. Even CEOs who discount the influence analysts have with them they put out the welcome mat. For one thing, information exchanged with analysts often is a two-way street: Analysts are ready sources for information about developments in the industry; they relay the thinking of investors; and they may express informed judgments about such things as stock repurchases and Internet investments.

According to analyst Peter Appert of Deutsche Bank Alex Brown, analysts at one point raised questions with Knight Ridder management about the *Philadelphia Inquirer*, because it was well-known that it was underperforming, with margins of six to seven percent. It may have been no coincidence that, after editor Gene Roberts departed the Inquirer, he pointedly commented:

"It is no secret that American newspapers increasingly have come under the control of corporate chains–many of them publicly held and solicitous of Wall Street analysts who see no newspaper obligations other than to the bottom line. . . .[Chain] ownership has

---

[26] For an account of the June 1999 Mid-Year Media Review, see memo, Appendix B.

become so pervasive that giant corporations pipe the tune to which most of journalism marches.... With the exception of a tiny handful of papers, the talk at the highest levels of newspapers these days is of increasing profits, increasing corporate pressure, increasing responsibility to shareholders."[27]

Appert said investors are much less focused than analysts on such individual papers as the *Inquirer*, but they hear about them from the analysts. An inescapable consequence of becoming a public newspaper company, therefore, is to come under the scrutiny of Wall Street functionaries whose allegiance is not to readers or to communities served by a company's papers–indeed, analysts seldom or never set foot in the cities–but to big brokerage customers who are far removed from the publications, and whose interests are strictly monetary.

Appert and other highly-regarded analysts who follow the newspaper industry–among them, Kevin Gruenich, Lauren Fine, Douglas Arthur, Mary Ann Winter, William Bird, Michael Kupinski and William Drewry–are names unfamiliar to editors but they nevertheless can have a big influence on their budgets, staffing and the kind of papers they produce by virtue of their own publications –their periodic reports, primarily to institutional investors, advising whether to buy, sell or hold particular newspaper stocks.

Analysts keep tabs on the industry and individual companies, build financial models and stay in close touch with corporate bigwigs. Although all but one of the publicly traded newspaper companies are heavily invested in newspapers, the analysts we interviewed do not systematically study the papers. They told us they read the national dailies, but see others only when they travel. A recent glowing report on Gannett, in which the analyst for a major brokerage issued a strong "buy" recommendation for Gannett stock, focused heavily on earnings and earnings per share, but paid no notice to the quality of the company's papers. (Not long thereafter, Gannett stock, which had languished in the low 60's, moved to the mid-70's.

---

[27] *"Corporatism vs. Journalism,"* The Press-Enterprise Lecture Series, Number 31, Feb. 12, 1996, P.J.

These are comments we received when we asked analysts how much weight, if any, they give to newspaper quality:

"Not a lot" of attention to quality. "The stock market is concerned about growth rate, not about quality. The market doesn't care." –William Drewry, Donaldson Lufkin and Jenrette.

"[I give] some weight to quality, but quality doesn't determine whether people read. I pay attention if the quality is very poor–the bottom line will be hurt; if the quality is very good, it could help, but by and large I pay attention to financials not quality." –Lauren Fine, Merrill Lynch.

"You sort of look at that but you have to look at quality of the finances. . . . In the case of companies with poorer quality papers, what counts with shareholders is if they make money. So quality is not a concern short-term if the company is profitable, but it would be a concern long-term." – Mary Ann Winter, Brown Brothers Harriman.

"Ads follow audience, so if the audience falls because quality isn't there, that's important. Pulitzers catch my eye, but quality isn't gauged on any one basis. It's a marginal issue because no one paper gives so much to the bottom line." –Kevin Gruenich, Bear Stearns.

Only one analyst, Appert of Deutsche Bank Alex. Brown, unequivocally accorded weight to quality, because "it will be helpful in circulation and advertising." However, he doesn't evaluate editorial quality as such or regularly examine a company's papers, though he believes editorial quality will be reflected in finances, because "financial measures depend on non-financial measures." Nevertheless, he said, he considers primarily financial criteria– earnings and cash flow.

The marginal part played by quality in analyst assessments irritates at least one CEO. Anthony Ridder, chairman and CEO of Knight Ridder, told us how he finds it "frustrating that they don't care about quality. Pulitzers? They couldn't care less. They want quality but they'd be much happier if we had Gannett margins; they'd jump with joy if we said we'd have Gannett margins, but we can't ignore our other constituents."

Newspaper company CEOs by and large expressed support for the idea that investment in quality–in newshole, staffing, salaries and training—would benefit the bottom line. The stock analysts tended to be skeptical:

• It depends what the papers do with bigger staffs and newsholes; if quality translates into more business, yes; otherwise not;

• The average person is not looking for quality—if the price of quality is too high, they will get "pissed;"

• Quality pays generally, but investment in the right areas is all important, and foreign bureaus are a wrong place to invest, as is sending too many people to cover the same event.

The way to a stock analyst's heart, therefore, is not simply to produce prize-winning journalism; consistently superior work would have to be done at reasonable cost and, preferably, be a revenue-enhancer.

Not surprisingly, that hard-headed approach has filtered into newsrooms. An editor told us how, several months after he had put more resources into improving a local feature, he was required to demonstrate a payoff in ad revenue or circulation.

The stock analysts we encountered are bright, hard-working, well-informed about the newspaper business, and respected by newspaper company executives. They are also mindful that newspapers aren't an ordinary business, that they have a public-service role in their communities. That said, the bottom line is that it's the bottom line that counts. We were told repeatedly by the analysts that they evaluate newspaper companies strictly as businesses, that the companies are judged without reference to the First Amendment, that no slack is cut because newspapers play a special informing role in society. As Lauren Fine of Merrill Lynch declared: "The second they became a public company, they became like any other business."

And like any other business where values are measured ultimately by stock price, the views of newspaper company stock analysts carry weight. Here is how several of the analysts sized up their impact:

• "We have tremendous influence on the companies. More than we should." Companies are "very stock-price conscious" and pay close attention to what analysts say. Investors pay attention to the consensus of analysts, so collectively analysts are very influential also with investors. Analysts have a big influence on stock prices in the short term, but on long-term price the analysts do not matter.

- Analysts have "lots of influence" on the direction of stock prices; "some influence" on company management and their decisions, but "not a huge influence" on them as companies "don't live or die" by what stock analysts say; nonetheless the analysts carry weight with management.
- Have "fair degree" of influence with investors and "more influence" with management now than earlier, as management is "trying to drive" the stock price.
- "A lot of influence" with investors, "some" influence with company management, "none" with the public. "Not much" influence by individual analysts, but "quite a lot" of influence collectively if there is a consensus.
- "Pretty high" level of influence. "More influential" with investors than with management, but "might be" influential there, too. Have influence also as a conduit of information from investors to management about how they regard the company.
- "A fair amount of influence." The analyst determines how "the world views" management. He has access to managers, who pay attention to his criteria.

Whether analyst influence on newspaper companies is adjudged "tremendous" or "fair" or somewhere in between, it's evident that the people who spend full-time evaluating behavior of the companies believe that their judgments are accorded at least respect by the companies and possibly affect their conduct.

A key issue on which analysts express themselves, and on which they presumably carry weight, is how much attention to pay to short-term and to long-term developments. Quarterly estimates by analysts are widely publicized and each company's actual quarterly results are compared to the estimates. Companies that greatly exceed or fall short of estimates can expect to read about it in the business news and find it reflected in the stock tables. When a single analyst for a major brokerage reduced the estimated quarterly earnings for Time Warner in August 1999, the company's shares lost about 7 percent, and more than 15 million shares changed hands.

The short-term, long-term issue is important to journalism because of the frequent ups and downs of the newspaper business. When newsprint prices rise or an economic downturn cuts into advertising revenue, excessive concern about the "next quarter" can lead to quick fixes on the cost side in the form of hiring freezes, downsizing and cutbacks in newshole, travel and training. Fewer reporters and copy editors and reduced news coverage almost always detract from a newspaper's quality. How much weight analysts and the investors they service give to short-term factors, therefore, can have a direct bearing on what happens in newsrooms across the country.

The analysts regard their primary audience as the money-manager clients of their brokerage houses. If a client is short-term oriented, the analyst necessarily has to provide guidance on the short-run outlook for particular companies, regardless of the preference an analyst may have to stress the long-term value of an investment. We were told repeatedly that institutional investors tend to have a very short-run focus. One analyst, who defined short-term as 12-18 months and long-term as 3 to 5 years, joked that the focus of institutional investors is "12 to 18 hours."

We asked analysts how much attention they give to short-term developments and to long-term. Here are responses:

William Drewry, of Donaldson, Lufkin and Jenrette–His focus is short-term "more than I like, because the stock market has a short focus," and he has to be mindful of that.

Mary Ann Winter, of Brown Brothers Harriman–She looks at both short-term and long-term prospects. She agreed that institutional investors are regarded as short-term oriented, but doesn't agree entirely that they are. It depends on the philosophy of the money managers; they have varied styles for managing money–some will buy and trade three days later, others hold for the long term. Because there are different philosophies for investing, she rates for short-term and long-term, but she prefers to recommend things that have long-term value, as long-term prospects also affect value in the short term.

Lauren Fine, of Merrill Lynch–Described herself as "more of a long-term person," and therefore did not downgrade McClatchy because of its acquisitions. Certainly, she said, some institutional investors are short-term, and her reports give both short-term and long-term ratings.

Peter Appert, of Deutsche Bank Alex. Brown–Believes institutional investors think short term, but also keep their eye on longer term–six months to several years, but not as long as 10. Investors in newspaper stocks tend not to be short-term. Nevertheless, they do keep management's feet to the fire for short-term results.

Kevin Gruenich, of Bear Stearns–Short-term results could affect the long-term outlook and, therefore, are important to the long run, but he leans heavily on short-term results because institutional investors think short-term. Because of them, he "absolutely" takes into account such short-term factors as the shifting price of newsprint.

Douglas Arthur, of Morgan Stanley Dean Witter–Gives 50-50 weight to a company's short-term and long-term prospects, but he is "relatively short-term oriented." He will not recommend a stock if it is not going to perform in six months to a year, the same time frame he ascribes to institutional investors.

It's evident that, whether they like it or not, analysts are captive of the interest by at least some of their institutional investors in short-term results, so that even a self-described "long-term person" has to heed quarterly thinking. It's not surprising, therefore, that virtually all of the newspaper company executives who spoke to analysts and investors at the Mid-Year Media Review in June 1999 made a point of citing their quarterly results. A few, notably Donald Graham, CEO of the Washington Post Co., openly disdained "quarterly thinking," and many subsequently told us of their commitment to long-term goals; still, given the quick-return objectives of some big investors and the consequent attention given to it by analysts, newspaper company managers have to be at least mindful of how good their balance sheets look in the short run. A major upshot of becoming a publicly traded newspaper company, therefore, is pressure for measures to produce short-term gains. To the extent that companies bend to the pressure, the price can be shorthanded newsrooms, and subtle and sometimes marked loss of newspaper quality.

Has "going public" then been good or bad for journalism? We put that question to analysts who follow the newspaper industry.

Considering that their livelihoods are tied to the decisions to "go public," we expected that they would be partial to the moves. Surprisingly, most took a dim view of the impact of Wall Street on journalism:

- It's hard to make a case that it's a positive for journalists or journalism, because "it forces a focus on financial objectives." On balance, it's not a good thing, as expenses have to be watched to achieve goals. Family-owned papers are tied to their communities, and those owners respond better to peer pressure in their communities to put out good papers.

- On balance, going public has been bad for journalism because of worry about the bottom line, and what you pay people. "Newspapers serve a wonderful purpose, so when you worry about the bottom line there's a big difference in what you do."

- "It probably has had a negative impact on journalism." Going public forces management to tighten the belt, "to come out of the ivory tower," to invest less in editorial. Staffs are leaner and there is less investigative reporting. The quality of newspapers has degraded, and part of that is due to going public. There have been cutbacks in publicly traded businesses generally, and newspapers are now in that same boat.

- Going public has created greater financial discipline, and that hasn't hurt the New York Times or Washington Post Companies, but it has created a quandary for smaller companies, and this analyst suspects that their journalism quality has suffered.

- The impact of going public has been negative. It creates more pressure on the bottom line, more pressure not to antagonize major advertisers. Privately-owned papers are freer to do what they want. Public companies have greater access to capital, and having stock is important for acquisitions, but going public, on balance, is more negative than positive.

- Going public has benefitted companies by giving them access to capital for better production (presses), and to fund growth. The price paid is increased scrutiny of financial results, but the days of quasi-charitable, public-trust newspapers have passed. On balance, the accessibility of capital makes going public a net plus.

- The suggestion that going public produced capital for investment in presses was rebutted by an analyst as "bogus" because "newspaper companies generate enough cash for that and never go into capital markets for that purpose."

The strong consensus among analysts that going public has been harmful to journalism is significant considering the source. These are not journalistic purists. While they do not systematically examine the press, and quality figures little in their judgments, they peer closely into the companies and know what makes them tick. Their collective judgment that what they see bodes ill for journalism is one of the more noteworthy findings of our study.

E. The CEOs

Newspaper company chief executives often meet with stock analysts and investors and are responsive to them to varying degrees. For the view from the top, we sampled more than half of the CEOs. When asked to define their constituents, not surprisingly, seven of the 10 CEOs cited stockholders. Most also said they had multiple constituencies; the most prominently mentioned among these were readers, advertisers, employees, and communities where the companies operate. Louis A. Weil III, then of Central Newspapers, described his "split constituency" as "Wall Street and Main Street," and added, "You have to pay more attention to Main Street."

Here is how the CEOs defined their obligation to stockholders:

"To grow the company; to earn a suitable return on their investment." William Burleigh, Scripps.

"They own the company and invested in it. We certainly owe it to them to run the business well for long-term investors; that will benefit all the company's constituents." Gary B. Pruitt, McClatchy.

"My mandate from the board is to produce longtime shareholder value." Robert Jelenic, Journal Register.

"I absolutely have a very large obligation to shareholders, an obligation to increase the value of the business, the long-term value. It doesn't get me off the hook simply to say increase profits; for 25 years we've been influenced by Warren Buffet, and our theory of our obligation is not real different from his, and in his annual report you never see reference to value per share." Donald Graham, Washington Post.

"If we serve readers-viewers, employees, and advertisers well, we will serve our shareholders well. The ultimate obligation is to shareholders, but we serve them best by serving the other three groups." Stewart Bryan, Media General.

"You have to perform well as a company. If you're not producing a good product, you're not producing decent profits. The only way to produce a fair return is through good products." –Louis A. Weil III, Central Newspapers.

"Make sure [shareholders] get the fair return they're entitled to." Anthony Ridder, Knight Ridder.

"My obligation is to increase the investment of shareholders at an above-average rate." Kenneth Madigan, Tribune.

"My first obligation is to take a longer view to build shareholder value and I want to out-perform peers in creating long-term value." Robert Woodworth, Pulitzer.

"To produce a healthy, competitive return." Peter Kann, Dow Jones.

The contacts CEOs have with investors were described variously as "a fair amount," "lots" with family and annually with others, "quite a bit," "twice a year," "an average of an hour a week," "constantly," "not a great deal," "frequently," "a significant amount a high priority."

While most CEOs make themselves accessible and hear investors out, they say they are not necessarily influenced by what they hear. Burleigh of Scripps said bluntly, "If investors don't like the way things are going, they can sell their shares and move on." Pruitt of McClatchy said he listens "but ultimately we need to decide what is in the long-term interest of the company…We don't want short-term investors." Graham of the Post said he pays "not much" attention to investor concerns.

But then, Bryan of Media General said he pays "lots of attention. It would be foolhardy to ignore investors. It makes a big impression if several suggest the same thing." But, he added, "I won't necessarily do it." Madigan of Tribune Co. also pays "a lot" of attention to investors. "It's very important to us. We're very focused on it."

Kann of Dow Jones pays a "fair amount" of attention; it's "worth a lot of his effort," but, as with virtually all of the other CEOs, Kann does not concede that the effort to pay attention to investors means that he follows in lockstep with them.

All of the CEOs meet with stock analysts, and they exchange information. Typically, the analysts obtain information about company performance and give their views on such things as industry trends, stock repurchases and newsprint prices. CEOs expressed varying views about the influence of analysts:

- "I listen to what analysts report and crank it into decision-making. I pay attention to their buy-sell-hold recommendations and won't get mad if we're downgraded. Analysts generally are not arbitrary. Other CEOs pay some sort of attention to them. The feeling is that they're fair, and attention is given out of respect." Burleigh, E.W. Scripps.

- "They have quite a bit of influence in general. They don't affect my decisions, but I don't ignore what they say, either, because what they say can influence the stock price, and I have to serve the interests of shareholders. That's different from tailoring your actions to the current thinking of stock analysts." Pruitt, McClatchy.

- "They're more of a benefit to stockholders than to me." Jelenic, Journal Register.

- "Their reports [about the company] get some internal attention, but I pay attention to our stockholders, not to the analysts." Graham, Washington Post.

- "They have some influence with me, but not very much. Some CEOs are very influenced by analysts, some not. Some do analysts' work for them–that is, provide them with a great deal of detail–because the CEOs are driven by much more fealty toward the concept of shareholder ownership only, not the interests of readers and employees. Most analysts think short-term; if you do that, you'll lose readers and not get them back. We serve them better if we let short-term profits slide sometimes." Bryan, Media General.

• "You want them to give you a buy recommendation, so you do care if they say sell the stock. You care how they feel. Generally it's stimulating to talk to them; they have good questions. It's frustrating that they don't care about quality." Ridder, Knight Ridder.

• "Analysts have a lot of influence. People listen to them. I pay a lot of attention, and the industry as a whole does, too." Madigan, Tribune.

• "They have a fair degree of influence with me and with the industry. They're smart; we ought to pay attention." Woodworth, Pulitzer.

• "Some analysts have good understanding, so I read their reports carefully and learn from them. Others are less credible." Kann, Dow Jones.

• "They have very little influence with the industry in general, but it depends on the company; the Washington Post doesn't care, others court the analysts. I feel an obligation to keep them informed, but they won't necessarily influence what the company does." Weill, Central.

Inasmuch as CEOs meet regularly with investors and analysts, and on the whole say they pay a fair degree of attention to both, the short-term outlook attributed to investors and analysts might be expected to be reflected in the way CEOs describe how they manage their companies. Nevertheless, about half of the CEOs say their focus is not quarter-to-quarter, but long-term. As Bryan of Media General put it, "Short-term thinking holds very little water with us."

Others said the interest in short-term results "is one of the factors you have to plug in;" "you can't ignore the short run but have to do what's best in the end;" "I spend a lot of time thinking about each quarter; I would like it if it weren't that way, but that's the way the game is played-we have to produce short-term results."

The "way the game is played" includes well-publicized quarterly earnings reports and stories about how far companies exceed or fall short of analyst estimates. Unless a newspaper company is fortunate to have substantial and loyal family ownership of publicly traded stock, or institutional investors who are unusually patient, a poor quarterly showing can be devastating to the company's stock price. So no matter how dedicated in theory company managers may be to building long-term value, for the most part they cannot be oblivious to the short-term measures necessary to protect the stock price.

Indeed, without exception, the CEOs said they pay close attention to their companies' stock price, with most checking it once or more daily. Madigan of Tribune Co., who looks "at it every day," has a Bloomberg machine on his desk and can look at it all day. While not "preoccupied [with the stock price]," Madigan said, "it's there." Others keep tabs on the stock price every day "because it's a barometer of how investors view the company," or because if something unusual happens to the price the CEO needs to know why.

Several, notably Pruitt of McClatchy, Graham of Washington Post and Kann of Dow Jones, downplayed the attention they give to short-term swings and emphasized long-term growth in their stock's value. Pruitt said he does not want to maximize his company's stock price short-term, as that's not in McClatchy's long-term interests. Graham cited Warren Buffet's belief that the stock market is in one sense a voting machine and in another sense a weighing machine. Graham says he pays attention to the stock price in the weighing machine sense–that is, the underlying value of the company. Said Kann of Dow Jones, "Ultimately, everything we do relates to getting the stock price up long-term."

Most of the CEOs have a personal financial interest in their company's stock price by virtue of their stock options.[28] Not surprisingly, the executives expressed satisfaction with the extent to which compensation is tied to stock price. Pruitt of McClatchy, who said one-third of his compensation is geared to his company's stock price, said that it's right to have a substantial part of compensation determined that way because of a CEOs obligation to stockholders, but that it should be related to long-term value of the stock.

Weill of Central Newspapers was in a distinct minority when he observed, "You can't control the stock price; it doesn't make sense to tie compensation to it." Weill said that, at his company, compensation incentives are related to earnings per share rather than

---

[28] For a detailed discussion with editors of executive compensation incentives, see Chapter IV, *infra*.

stock price. Nevertheless, Weill said he watched Central's stock price daily.

It's evident that, whether or not newspaper company managers profess to be interested in stock price primarily over the long haul, they cannot be indifferent to it on a day-to-day basis. One of the consequences of "going public," therefore, is the central role the stock market comes to play in the company. Newspapers may be a "different kind of business," but in that regard they become very much like any other publicly owned business, especially those which attempt to align the interests of managers with those of stockholders by way of stock-price-related incentives.

Does investment in quality pay off on the bottom line and, ultimately, in stock price? The CEOs by and large were emphatic that it does. But there were cautions and caveats:

• Burleigh of Scripps and Kann of Dow Jones said that investing in bigger newshole would be of no value unless the space is filled with quality content. Burleigh called it a "delicate balancing act" to obtain a good return on investment and to put out quality papers.

• Weill of Central Newspapers said it "depends on each individual operation - more is not necessarily better. I've seen it go both ways. Just opening up the newshole doesn't make a good paper."

• Madigan of Tribune Co. said, "If [investment in quality] brings readers and advertisers, then it is; it depends on whether readers want quality. If they don't, and editors want it, then it's a drain on the bottom line. In the end, though, having good newspapers and a reputation for good journalistic values will be rewarded ultimately by Wall Street."

• Woodworth of Pulitzer described himself as a big believer in the "lifeboat theory–there's a maximum number of people in a lifeboat to get ashore, but not one more. A paper with 380 people is not necessarily better than one with 350. The key is to grow ad linage. That will grow the newshole, help revenue and increase circulation."

• That investment in quality pays has been the long-time belief at the Washington Post, said CEO Graham: "No two ways about it. But will it be true in the future with the Web challenge for ads? The belief here [at the Post] is that readers will continue to reward quality, but personally, as for the future, I'm not sure."

• Pruitt, of McClatchy, one of the few companies explicitly to tie CEO compensation to quality, said: "Many companies are concerned about quality, but very few have it discussed at the very highest level, as McClatchy does, by the CEO and the board. To view quality and stock price as tradeoffs is to look short-term." Pruitt added that circulation growth reflects quality, and is the best indicator of a paper's long-term future. "At McClatchy, circulation accounts for at least 20 percent of publisher and editor bonuses. That's part of why we do better on circulation than others."

Is public ownership of newspaper companies good or bad for journalism? CEOs gave a mixed verdict:

• Burleigh, Scripps–"It's been good for this company. It forced us to accept the discipline of the marketplace. It gave us confidence that we could run with the gazelles, unlike the days when the company was run very paternalistically. As for the industry as a whole, it's a mixed bag; in some towns papers were made better, but in some towns the vital presence of the paper in the community lessened with absentee ownership. Overall, the result of going public is not black and white."

• Pruitt, McClatchy–"It's hard to give a definite answer, but for those companies that focus on short-term Wall Street response that focus is bad for journalism. Newspaper companies have the luxury other companies don't have because of substantial family investment, which enables them to be longer-term. Publicly traded companies focused short-term will do a disservice to journalism, but the disservice is not necessarily a byproduct of being a public company. It all depends on the issue of focus, long-term or short-term. The scrutiny that you get being a public company brings professionalism and sharpness that can be valuable, and being public allows use of stock as currency for acquisition."

• Robert Jelenic, Journal Register–"It's been good for journalism. In our case, it added capital to grow the company. It gave us resources to do a $300 million acquisition of a chain that we made better–more pages, more staff, and color. It's been good for the companies I'm familiar with, and I can't think of a bad example.

Generally, if you have resources to add such things as presses, then it's a plus for the industry."

• Donald Graham, Washington Post–"There's no magic in any form of ownership. Some very good papers are public, some very good are private, and there are terrible in each. The discipline instilled by being a public company is a good thing."

• Stewart Bryan, Media General–"It's a mixed bag. If all papers stayed private, there would be some bad papers. On the other hand, good papers went bad after they went public. Our company went public in 1966 and I believe our journalism is better."

• Louis Weil III, Central Newspapers–"Going public requires management to pay careful attention to a lot of constituents it hadn't paid attention to before. On balance, it's been a plus for us."

• Anthony Ridder, Knight Ridder–"I have to answer in two ways: Newspapers are better, and the best are owned by public companies; they tend to attract better people, there's more professionalism, and the journalism is better. There is profit pressure, but it hasn't hurt the journalism. The other part of the answer is that you have to worry month-to-month, quarter-to-quarter, when revenue isn't growing, so you have to take tougher action, do more on the revenue side."

• Kenneth Madigan, Tribune Co.–"It's been good for journalism; it brings sound discipline that a lot of companies didn't have before they went public. It's been a real plus for our company. Before 1983, when we went public, we weren't held in very high regard either as a business or journalistically. Going public has brought a sense of urgency to improve."

• Robert Woodworth, Pulitzer–"The downside is that public companies focus too heavily on short-term results to the detriment of communities and readers. There's also a lot of regimentation in some public companies - a formulaic approach. On the upside, because of obligations to shareholders, they're much stronger financially. On the whole, it's been beneficial."

• Peter Kann, Dow Jones–"Nothing is without some negatives, but by and large newspapers are better publicly controlled. Some of the very best, such as the *New York Times*, *Washington Post* and *Wall Street Journal*, have significant family ownership but others that don't are perfectly good. There also are bad publicly owned papers and bad papers that aren't."

Recall that stock analysts who follow the newspaper industry were almost uniformly negative about the consequences to journalism of the decision to go public. The CEOs we sampled could be expected to be more upbeat about the business arrangements under which they operate, and they were. But it's noteworthy that they also expressed a certain degree of ambivalence about being a Wall Street commodity. Considering the source, that signals a noteworthy degree of unease about the downside to journalism of becoming a Wall Street product.

F. The Omnipresence of the Investment Market

Much of the foregoing has to be seen in the context of a changed investment environment. Investment markets, and institutional investors, were not, until recently, large objects on the radar screen. It has not been until the last 20 or fewer years that the current environment has emerged. Features of that environment are: great increases in the amount of equity investment capital; remarkable broadening of the portion of the population that participates in those markets; and management of these expanding investment assets, in increasing proportion, by widely held mutual funds, investment-banking organizations, insurance companies, and pension plans. The new forces of broad participation in the equity markets and institutional fund managers have made the markets much more sensitive to corporate performance, much more exclusively focused on financial performance of companies, especially in the relatively short run, and ironically much less liquid for the large institutional investors.

The institutional investors own large stakes in companies, the rapid sale of which will affect share prices. This is particularly so because other institutional investors with their own large stakes tend to react as a group: If one sells and the sale may affect price, many will attempt to sell also to reduce their losses and exposure. The institutional investors live quarter by quarter and are not in a good position to take the long-term view (Warren Buffet is a rare exception), for other mutual funds are competing for investment money, and the trustees of the pension and other managed funds are watching quarterly performance and making decisions about whether to stay with one manager or move to another. In terms of market performance and market expectations, especially as they bear on the companies whose stock is owned, the institutional investors form a block of ownership that is in many ways monolithic, even if the 50- or 60-percent institutional ownership is held by 10 or 20 or 30 different institutional investors. And the institutional investors not only demand short-term performance; they are also forced because of their inability to quickly sell and shift large investments, to make that demand known to the companies, to insist on management policies that will accomplish that end, and to put pressure (in indirect but effective ways) on the companies, their management or boards to be responsive to their interests and concerns.

Added to this mix have been two changes in the regulatory environment. The first is a general loosening of the ability of investors–institutional investors being most prominent because most organized, informed, and interested–to communicate their preferences to the companies. This can be done now in informal (and therefore more direct and effective) ways. In the past, any real pressure had to be exerted through annual meetings and proxy contests, which were almost never effective, were way too slow to achieve results, and in any event couldn't address operational matters in the hands of the management and boards. Today the communications directly with companies are open–indeed, with the disclosure requirements and the strict limits on inside information, openness to communication is almost a necessity.

The second, and perhaps more important, change is the ability of institutional investors to speak among themselves, to join forces (informally) and present a united front. The ability of such large investors to communicate among themselves has now been legally approved by the SEC rules. This apparently minor change has had very large consequences: CEOs and CFOs now feel obliged to communicate regularly with investors, in meetings and one on one; and on the other side, a more united and coherent message *from* the institutional investors to the companies has resulted. While institutional investors are not permitted (without great tax and other penalties) to act in formal concert with one another if their combined interest in a company's shares would exceed five percent, the ability to communicate permits concerted action in many informal but perhaps no less effective ways.

Finally, the stock analysts who work for institutional investors or for large brokerage companies have great influence on stock price. The influence may well be magnified because of the concern of the institutional investors with the analysts' assessments. Those assessments can influence market demand fairly quickly, sometimes dramatically, and can thus significantly influence the returns that institutional investors must achieve and report on a quarterly basis. It is interesting, though not surprising in light of all of this, that the CEOs most often refer to meetings with analysts; to how good the analysts' questions are; to how smart they are; to how useful their advice and insight can be (though the CEOs don't always follow it).

Two things should be said about the analysts. First, their questions and criticisms and suggestions go directly to operational matters (staffing, circulation, revenue growth, margins, etc.–i.e. to the heart of business decisions which, it will be recalled, are matters that previously could not even be raised as proposals at shareholder meetings). Second, their advice is typically directed primarily, if not exclusively, at strictly financial measures–debt load, debt service, balance sheet condition, profit and operating income, capital requirements, acquisitions and divestitures, etc.–that bear on current and future stock price. This is the stuff of the fabled Harvard MBAs, abstracted from the day-to-day business of a company producing and selling product to consumers, and instead focused on the financial measures of the company as a return-maximizing investment.

It is in this broader context of a changed investment environment and altered expectations for publicly traded companies that what the CEOs are saying must be interpreted. The differences among them are generally minor. In only a few cases are there fairly stark differences, and even then only on emphasis and message to the investment community, not on responsiveness to its ultimate investment interests. The CEOs, almost without being aware of it, are all captive to the gravitational force of the investment market. If one argues for a bit more long-term thinking, another for journalistic quality and health, etc., these differences are ultimately little more than incidental and insignificant, for all of these comments are made against the background of obligation to the ends of the financial marketplace. They are variations only on the same general theme: Maximize return and shareholder value for a shareholder community whose interest is in market price and financial return, not in the business in which any company is engaged, and whose investment decisions occur in a highly liquid marketplace of competing investments.

It is, therefore, not surprising that few and narrow differences would be found among the CEOs. They are at the point of contact between the company and the investment marketplace, and they can't operate in any context other than one that responds to the demands of that marketplace.

Has going public been good for news and journalism? Yes, some say, because it has made newspapers leaner and stronger organizations. True. But leaner and stronger in what sense? Not in terms of the public goals of the companies as providers of news and information, but in terms of financial strength and the capacity to produce even greater profits in the future. Quality, strength, and efficiency in the public companies have become, by legal, economic, and structural necessity, standards going to financial performance and not to news. Beneath the particular responses of the CEOs is another message about a cultural milieu, a set of priorities and values in which the CEOs operate and which are, in themselves, the most revealing facts. The business of news is business, not news.

Chapter IV

Organizational Behavior and Dynamics In the Publicly Traded Newspaper Firm

A. Introduction

The ownership structures of the firm, the composition of the shareholders and the locus of shareholder control, the composition of the boards of directors, the outlook of executive management, and the incentive structures that are put in place, all constitute the organizational framework in which the day-to-day, year-to-year, operation of the firm takes place. In this chapter our interest is to move beyond the structures that characterize the ownership and incentive systems and to examine how these forces become manifest in the operation of the firm's business, and particularly in the oversight, management, and operation of the newspaper companies that, in combination, constitute the "business" of the firm. To do this we spoke with editors about how they and the news personnel actually function; we explored critical news and business decisions, such as circulation policies, to find out how and why they are made and carried out; and we examined the operating policies and arrangements in the firm, with specific attention to the forms of management control exacted by the parent company over the newspaper subsidiaries. From these and other pieces of the firm's operation we attempt to paint a picture of the newspaper business as practiced in the publicly traded firm today.

B. The Editors

The actions of directors, stock analysts, investors, and CEOs reverberate in newsrooms. It is there that editors have to work out their obligations to staff, to customers, to communities–and to corporate, which means, ultimately, to stockholders. For, as Mark Willes, then CEO of Times Mirror, phrased it, earning a rate of return investors consider adequate "is not a nice to do, it's a must do."

We examined how that "must do" sentiment is communicated by the parent corporation to local news organizations, and the editorial impact it has, by observing it through the eyes of editors. It is they, after all, who are directly responsible for editorial content, and they must serve, and balance the needs of, their papers' various constituencies. Increasingly, that means responding to the constellation of pressures from outside and from above by working closely with the business side.

James Naughton, a former editor who directs the Poynter Institute, described the altered status and role of editors this way:

"In the 1990s, an editor customarily is a member of the company's operating committee–a senior member, perhaps even an executive vice president, but only one in a panel of peers, all of whom have more in common with each other than with the editor. The editor, like the others on the operating committee, is preoccupied with consultant reports and focus groups and the search for the latest theory or device to recapture lapsed customers or, failing that, the least injurious way to trim costs and maintain margin. . . . The operating committee may have a dozen or more members. The editor's influence upon the others may be less the consequence of rank than of relationships–with the publisher, with the vice president for advertising, with the general counsel, with the director of marketing, with the human resources vice president. Some editors may still dominate corporate conversations about what constitutes news and how to deploy newsgatherers, but most no longer make such determinations singly or without elaborately justifying the effects on the bottom line."[29]

We interviewed 50 editors, selected at random from among newspapers owned by 15 of the publicly traded companies. To encourage candor, we pledged not to identify the editors. One editor

---

[29] *"The Business of News, the News About Business,"* Nieman Reports, Summer 1999 Special Issue.

declined the offer of anonymity but also subsequently declined to answer several questions.

We noted, at the outset, that there is much talk these days "about bottom-line pressures on editors," and asked, "Do you personally feel such pressure?" Ninety percent–all but five–responded affirmatively to one degree or another, with the affirming editors expressing varying degrees of acceptance, resignation or resentment. The responses:

"Yes. The paper has a fairly aggressive profit goal," which, the editor said, means fewer people and less operating money.

"Yes, but not in ways that directly affect journalism," because of a bigger staff and newshole. He feels "lots of pressure to meet the annual plan, and if we're off on the plan I have to stop spending money–to not fill a vacancy, for instance. There's a need to deliver high profits to Wall Street."

"Yes, I'm aware of financial constraints, but not unduly so."

"Absolutely, I feel bottom-line pressure, but that's not a negative. When I started, papers were considered a public trust–spend what you need. Now, they're a business, and you have to think about how to find resources, how to live within a budget, how to be a successful business."

"Yes, there's lots of pressure, which makes it very difficult on news coverage."

"No, I don't feel pressure because I have the money I need to run the newsroom." He added, "Of course, I can always use more."

"I've always felt pressure at papers where I've worked, though less here than elsewhere, but the trend of pressure is up."

"Yes, especially at the end of the fiscal year. The publisher won't say you can't do this or that, but you have to be aware of the need to meet the budget so you might not do things you'd do otherwise."

"There's much more pressure than there used to be when money would flow in over the transom, and especially since the paper became shareholder-owned. I have to be literate in business and more involved in marketing and circulation."

"No, I don't really feel bottom-line pressure. In any business, you can't spend money endlessly. I don't have the sense that I'd like to do the right thing but can't. Everyone can use more staff, but we're not prevented from doing a good job."

"I always have bottom-line pressure, primarily on staffing," in part because of transfer of production tasks to the newsroom.

"Yes, we recently went through downsizing for a bigger stockholder return. The newshole is holding its own for now but I suspect that will be reassessed."

"Yes, very directly, as we're going through downsizing to meet new profit margins."

"To a degree. Budgets must be met and they're never what you want them to be, but we haven't had to make major cutbacks."

"Yes, on full-time equivalents and color usage; there's less color on news pages if ads aren't there. I'm always looking at overtime issues and have to work smarter with fewer people. I sure do think of bottom line pressure; it's in the back of my mind."

"Yes, there's a hiring freeze on now. Always in the back of my mind is, am I making budget? I work for a company that makes a lot of money but it always wants more. It's frustrating that the targets are moving–you have a strategy and all of a sudden, if you don't hit targets, what you planned editorially is slashed to meet the numbers. You look and see that the economy is OK, so why? It's frustrating."

"I feel no bottom-line pressure. I've been in the business 30 years and there's no greater pressure now than at any other time. The paper has to make money."

"Yes. When newsprint costs went up, we froze hiring, cut positions, tightened the newshole, and eliminated a couple of weekly sections. When things got better on newsprint, we added staff and sections. Not daily pressure. It depends on if we're meeting budget; if we are, then things are fine; otherwise there's not as much travel, and positions are held open."

"I do feel pressure. It's easier to take when numbers continue to grow, as they do and I add resources. I spend no major time, maybe five percent, worrying about the budget. The pressure usually is how to figure out ways to improve coverage by reallocating resources rather than getting all I need."

"Sure I feel pressure. You can't get as much money as you want. I have to do my part for the company's financial performance, have to make budget, have to worry about it. I'm on the operating committee and feel budget pressure that way, too. It's a growing market, so there's pressure on how to keep up and get resources for growth."

"Oh, definitely. There's an operating-profit goal; I'm aware of it when money is not coming though the door. Staff has been cut and the training budget, too. We can't go to American Press Institute meetings or desirable conferences or seminars."

"Of course, everybody feels budget pressure. That's business. Everyone is affected by the bottom line. I'd like more, but I'm pretty happy with what we have."

"Of course. There's continuing stress on resources. It's not new–ever since newsrooms had budgets–but I'm more aware of it now. We are money sinks."

"I don't feel bottom-line pressure per se. I'm aware of the bottom line and aware that the status of the newsroom depends on the budget, so I feel the effects of the bottom line, but it cuts in both directions when profits are high."

"Yes. We're not doing what we should to draw readers. Penetration has declined because of an expenses-driven short-term orientation."

"I guess so, but it's not onerous, just part of the job, and it's not as bad as at my previous paper, which was individually owned, where the pressure was awful."

"Sure, especially on staffing. I have to make budget targets. The biggest cost is labor, so if I have to cut expenses, we will not fill vacancies, as we're doing now, as well as monitoring overtime and part-time."

"A tremendous amount of bottom-line pressure–everything from overtime, salaries, travel, everything that costs money–to get the profit margin up. The fear is that if they don't get the percentage up, the paper will be sold."

"[A]bsolutely [I] feel pressure. It's hard to be an editor nowadays without feeling it. I became an editor because I wanted to do journalism, but now it's about the bottom line. Staffing is an issue.

There's an obsession with FTEs [full time equivalents] and profit margins. It used to be that in a bad year, well, there's less to spend, but you can't keep chipping away at staff, can't do with less indefinitely. The company's mantra is you have to figure out what you can stop doing, but readers notice. We can't cover state news the way it needs to be done. It's frustrating."

"Sure, but that's not necessarily bad. It's silly for editors to be separated from business. Newsrooms have big expenses–newshole, the cost of newsprint. You have to have a place at the table."

"Yes, we just recently downsized and were told that next year general expenses can only be 1½ percent more. We're definitely feeling the heat, way beyond the control of anyone at the paper."

"Yes, there's pressure on hiring, use of resources, newshole, on virtually every dollar."

"Yes, I feel bottom-line pressure, but the good at this company outweighs the bad. In feeding shareholders they make lots of money. It's a balancing act, how much to stockholders, how much to the paper for such things as equipment. We're not doing anything horrible feeding the bottom line, but we have fewer reporters than comparable papers. I have a fantasy that I win the lottery, buy the paper and reduce the profit margin. I need a bigger newshole."

"Sure. Every editor does, and more so over the past 25 years. The pressure is on staffing and newshole. I don't feel a lot of pressure day-to-day, but there's month-to-month budget pressure. I felt it more at my previous paper, but it's growing more here on the expense side."

"Yes. Going public is the most significant newspaper development in the past 20 years. The impact of going public ends up in the newsroom in terms of productivity and the like; there's a direct line between Wall Street and the newsroom. Productivity determines how you allocate resources between journalism of general interest and local interest. There's intense market pressure to segment to sub-communities. That makes it harder to report on Community with a capital C vs. community with a small c."

"Yes, I just got the budget, and three positions were cut, a big hit. The newshole also was cut. Other departments were cut, but the newsroom was cut harder. The profit margin is close to 40 percent but the bottom-line pressure has been intense in the past year."

"Yes, I'm expected to meet budgets and control expenses. The emphasis on dollars causes reluctance to ask for things or to start up things that cost money. It creates a different attitude."

"Absolutely. I'm a company officer, so I have fiduciary responsibility to company and shareholders, and a responsibility to put out high-quality papers. The stated goal of the company is, No. 1, improve shareholder value. It talks about quality and wants to put out quality–it doesn't squeeze as others do, but it's subject to market forces."

"Yes. Independence of news from business is a thing of the past. Editors have less control."

"Yes. I have responsibility to make the budget and to make the company's budget. I also have MBO [Management By Objective] goals related to the budget. I'm an officer of the company, so I have fiscal responsibility also for that."

"Yes, especially in hiring. The amount I can pay and for raises is far too restrictive. They won't allow me to spend what's budgeted; if someone leaves, I can't shift the money. I have to accept more advertorial material; it's a constant battle."

"Sure. Every year it's a struggle to balance resources, to hold expenses to revenue, to do more with no more staffing."

"Sure, but 'pressure' implies that's bad. You have to recognize it's a business–you have to make profit, and high profit is expected by shareholders. I get monthly budget reports and have to monitor spending."

"No. I don't feel bottom-line pressure. I have profit targets, but it's not intense pressure. I'm not very aware of it because times are good and the company seems alert that quality papers are successful."

"Yes. I feel it in shaping the budget, a number we have to hit. I'm told to cut because expenses are high and revenue low. There's pressure to exceed the year before, definitely pressure. It shows in the newsroom when planning a zoned edition, expanding a bureau, when you can't do the things you plan to do. I can do a good job, but it's hard to expand. The bottom-line pressure on editors is extreme.

Credibility of the press is on the line because not enough resources are going into papers."

"Absolutely [I] feel pressure on staffing, ability to buy features, travel, everything."

"Absolutely. The last couple of years have been wonderful; [we] added staff and newshole. But profits have to increase each year, as it's a publicly traded company with stockholders, and we had to make cuts when newsprint prices were high and things were hot competitively."

"Oh, sure. Ever since papers discovered that readers could leave them, editors realized they have to be involved in circulation. Newsrooms are acutely aware of the need to pay attention also to advertising, to the revenue side of the paper. I wish the old days were here; they were a luxury. The pressure now is to retain readers and provide a format that works for advertisers–subjects, topics, an environment favorable for ads, adjacencies. It complicates the life of editors. Their need to think of the whole business has increased exponentially."

A recurring theme of the editors was concern about staffing. About 40 percent of them tied the financial pressure they experience primarily to belt-tightening on payroll, to "chipping away at staff." Notable in that connection was the extent to which editors expressed frustration at periodic staff and other cuts to meet moving revenue and profit targets–the demands placed on them, in other words, by virtue of the parent company's efforts to meet the short-term expectations of analysts and investors. The labor-intensive nature of newsrooms, coupled with the periodic ups and downs of the newspaper business, make the editorial side of newspapers especially vulnerable to the "next quarter" mentality. As one editor complained, "My company is too much quarter-to-quarter; it's not enough long-term, and it makes decisions harmful to the long-term franchise." The "direct line" that one editor saw between "Wall Street and the newsroom" was not a figment of his imagination; rather, it was a consequence of the reality of running a newsroom in an environment where the focus almost inescapably, and at times obsessively, is on stock price.

The editors we interviewed typically drew up the editorial budget initially, but corporate headquarters almost invariably had the last word, with local publishers and/or the local operating committee weighing in prior to corporate's review. A number of editors described corporate input at the outset in the form of "targets" or "expectations." Budget scrutiny at the corporate level ranged from cursory, with few questions asked, to intense. An editor described how one year corporate increased the newshole and how at other times some minor to moderate adjustments were made by corporate in the paper's favor, but now "there's tremendous pressure to increase the stock price." Another editor told how he first battles the publisher, who favors equipment over pay increases, and then corporate, "a micro-managing bunch" who set the newshole every month and scrutinize every part of the newsroom budget, including reporters' notebooks, ("I put in things they can cut out.") "I hope they buy more papers so they're too busy to nit-pick; they put me through agony. Why do you need this and need that?" Other editors cited corporate emphasis on FTEs and trimming positions.

Editors know their staffs, their capabilities and productivity, and the coverage needs of their communities. The frustration we encountered among editors is hardly surprising considering that decisions affecting their newsrooms frequently are made by people with short-term outlook who not only are distant from the local scene but whose objective is to pad already substantial profits to impress those who never even read the papers.

The editors were divided about whether editorial quality at their papers takes a back seat to meeting budget targets. Just under half said there had been no sacrifice of quality, though many quickly added they could always use more resources for newshole, staff and travel ("If I had buckets of money we could do better, but I can produce a quality paper with what I have"); some said that while they maintain quality now, they fear for the future.

The comments of the slightly more than half who said that quality is, indeed, compromised generally cited inadequate newshole, staff numbers, and salaries. Related complaints:

"Before, journalistic quality was the only consideration, now it's not." "The point corporate misses is how not proposing things because of cost inhibits creative thinking, and what it does to 'soul' – the really big things, the story you decide not to do in depth;" the constant turnover due to "atrocious" pay; the errors because you are short people on the copy desk; the stories that go uncovered because of vacancies that can't be filled, or because of the expense. "You write about car dealers very carefully; home builders also are big advertisers, so the publisher wants to see and soften those stories;" the staff's experience level reduced 50 percent in five years because of pay. "It's always been true that being a journalist is like being on an expedition every day, you make do with what you have," but there's "more quarterly pressure now" and delayed investment.

Nearly three-fourths of the editors we interviewed receive stock options, the potentially lucrative opportunity to exercise the option to buy stock a stipulated number of years later at the (presumably lower) price quoted for the stock at the time the option was granted. Surprisingly, most of the editors were mystified about the basis for the awards. Several speculated they were granted on the basis of title or the size of the paper or financial performance. The puzzled editor who said, "It beats the hell out of me," pretty much summed up the uncertainty most editors expressed about the reason for their awards.

Stock options are a device to align the interests of beneficiaries, usually top executives, with those of stockholders, on the theory that managers will do what they can to boost a stock's price because they personally stand to benefit. It's doubtful that editors are in position to have even minimal influence on a stock's behavior in the marketplace. And if they did have influence, it would be contrary to journalistic ethics for them to attempt to cash in on it. The Statement of Principles of the American Society of Newspaper Editors describes the obligation of editors this way:

"The primary purpose of gathering and distributing news and opinion is to serve the general welfare by informing the people and enabling them to make judgments on the issues of the time. Newspapermen and women who abuse the power of their professional role for selfish motives or unworthy purposes are faithless to that public trust."

Moreover, if the purpose of stock options were to incline editors to pay attention to the concerns of stockholders, it would be at odds with how editors regard their role. When we asked editors "to define your constituency," they responded virtually without exception that it was "readers." At times they mentioned "staff" or "advertisers" or "community" along with "readers," but "stockholders" were almost never cited except when editors noted that if they served readers well, stockholders also would benefit.

An editor commented: "I think of readers first and foremost. At times you think about corporate and stockholders, but reject that idea." Said another, "It doesn't enter my mind to think about stockholders or the parent company." Added a third, "Readers are why most of us got into this business–to do good while having fun." The prevailing view was summed up best by the editor who said, "I don't think of stockholders; increasing shareholder value is the company's goal, but not mine."

The apparent attempt to make it an editor's goal through stock options would appear to have missed the mark, to judge from what editors said when we asked whether they believe the options influence behavior. The virtually unanimous verdict: Stock options may serve as a retention device but do not otherwise affect their conduct.

An editor summed up his reaction to the influence of options by telling how, when he and other editors thought about overtime to cover a particular story and wondered how it might mess up the budget, "they looked at each other and said, 'Aw, fuck it! We're here to do a job.'" Others noted that "there's too much distance" between what they do and the stock price, or that "it never occurs to me that I'm making decisions that hurt the stock price" or that "I never look at the budget and say that if I cut more I'll benefit." Another editor said that he simply doesn't ever think about his stock options, and added, "They [corporate] probably think that's the problem with editors."

If the options do not necessarily produce the desired effect, it's nevertheless troubling that newspaper companies employ a device intended to put editors in tune with the interests of shareholders and that amounts to a conflict of interests. The fact that editors testify the options do not influence their decisions doesn't alter the potential of stock options to divide their loyalties. That would be especially true if options become a valuable and coveted part of compensation. And in at least some instances there is no doubt that options are important. For example, when the New York Times Company announced its intention to create a separate Internet company, editorial-staff holders of Times Company options became very interested in whether they would share in the new stock through their options, interested to the point of causing internal anxiety among editorial staff.[30] But whatever the value of stock options, it seems wrong in principle to put journalists in the position of being tempted, or appearing to be tempted, to feather their own nests to serve the interests of stockholders.

Stock options are a benefit with potential value. Bonuses, on the other hand, are of immediate benefit. All but one of the editors we interviewed was eligible for a bonus, and it could be sizable, as much as 20 percent or more of salary. Bonuses for editors typically are awarded under a Management by Objective (MBO) system for achieving objectives established jointly by the editor and his or her publisher, but some also may be set by corporate.

The bonuses of only a tiny minority of editors were tied strictly to meeting editorial objectives, such as establishing new sections, beefing up training, or increasing staff diversity. Some three-fourths had bonuses dependent on a mix of editorial and financial objectives, with as much as 90 percent of the bonus amount at times determined by financial factors. About 20 percent of editors received bonuses solely on the basis of financial yardsticks. Several editors volunteered that bonuses had shifted from rewards wholly or mostly for editorial performance to rewards tied primarily or altogether to meeting profit targets, staying under budget, or to other money measurements.

---

[30] See *Off The Record*, New York Observer, Aug. 2, 1999; *The Options Option*, P. 52, Columbia Journalism Review (May/June 2000).

The *American Journalism Review* described in detail the MBO of an unnamed senior editor at a Knight Ridder newspaper. Among the objectives for which the editor would be rewarded:

"To help [the paper] achieve its goal of increasing advertising revenue through shifts from competitors' share of the market, we will foster a relationship with the advertising division that results in a constant exchange of information on matters of mutual concern. These include special sections produced by the newsroom that might result in additional advertising; the opportunity to sell advertising adjacent to regular news features; and flexibility on our part, when appropriate, on the placement of advertising on pages with news content...."[31]

The editors we interviewed at times expressed irritation about their bonuses being affected by matters over which they had no control. One editor described the financial objectives established for her bonus as "repugnant." But another editor, who said the lion's share of his bonus was based on financial performance, shrugged it off. "Do I fill a position now? Do we go up a page? When those questions arise I'm not really thinking much about the bonus, and most of the people who work for me don't base actions on it. I'm not going to sacrifice editorial quality for dollars. You have to have an irreverent attitude toward spending money."

At least one ostensibly non-editorial objective arguably relates closely to content: circulation. Editors, unlike circulation directors, do not have responsibility to beat the bushes for readers, but how well a newspaper serves its community and readers can determine how many people buy it. Many editors told us, in fact, that circulation serves for them as an important measure of editorial quality. MBOs that include circulation among their components–as they sometimes do for editors–would be justified not just for editors but for CEOs and other high corporate officials, though seldom do compensation plans for higher-ups even mention circulation.

Dangling a reward for editors for higher circulation also does not have built-in the same conflict as other incentives. When an

---

[31] *Management by MBO (Part 2)*, American Journalism Review, Dec. 1998, p. 64.

editor's bonus depends on staying at or below the budgeted newshole or at or below budgeted FTE levels, as is often the case, editors may be forced to choose between serving readers or their own financial interest.

James Naughton of the Poynter Institute told the *American Journalism Review* how the MBO has become an "insidious process" that makes editors "unduly conscious or even subconscious of their own potential gain at the risk of something that they might otherwise want to do in the newsgathering process. I don't think people sit there and pull out their MBO charts and say in October, 'How many things do I need to kill to make a bigger bonus?' But I do think the existence of that process in a newsroom setting, where historically we have prided ourselves on being separate from profit-makers, has changed the perception among editors. And it has spread throughout the newsroom, to department heads, which may be draining their enthusiasm to bust the budget when they oughta by God bust the budget because the news is important."[32]

Bonuses for editors geared to profit targets or to other non-editorial objectives thus can be inimical to the interests of readers. When bonuses are coupled with stock options, the mix can be especially toxic to the professionalism of journalists as well.

C. Circulation

Geneva Overholser, a former Gannett editor, has written: "Walk into any sizable newsroom in the country, ask where you can find the editor, and chances are good the answer will be: in the Marketing Committee. It's the place today where key decisions affecting newsrooms are made–how to boost circulation, how to create new sections, how to structure zoned coverage, how to define the paper's target audience. Editors spend long hours with their counterparts from advertising, marketing and circulation, and they are being pushed to turn news coverage toward the most profitable

---

[32] Geneva Overholser, *Editor Inc.*, American Journalism Review, Dec. 1998, p. 58.

territory: the interests of women, younger readers, suburbanites, and the affluent."[33]

Overholser's comment about the tilt of news coverage "toward the most profitable territory" is reflected in the experience of Maxwell E. P. King, former editor of Knight Ridder's *Philadelphia Inquirer*. King recounted in 1998 how the *Inquirer* lost 70,000 daily readers and 100,000 Sunday readers over the last 15 years. Even though the losses amounted to 14 percent of daily readership and 10 percent of Sunday readers, King reported that there were no complaints from advertisers or from the paper's own ad executives. His explanation: the losses were almost all from lower-income neighborhoods.[34]

"Although the *Inquirer* had lost gross circulation numbers," said King, "its demographic statistics–the wealth, education, and other characteristics of our reading population–had improved substantially. In fact, although we lost circulation badly in the city, we have been gaining circulation in the wealthier suburban neighborhoods. . . . Most of our advertisers were pretty happy about the readers we were delivering."

Their advertisements helped support new *Inquirer* sections for affluent suburbia. The result, said King, is that "the city neighborhoods and the poorer sections of our region are getting coverage that is not even close to the suburban . . . coverage. The economic pressures inexorably push the newspaper toward more detailed coverage of sectors with the sort of demographics that support the effort."

What King described in Philadelphia also is true, he said, "of most of the big, successful metropolitan newspapers," which "are relentlessly moving upscale, becoming the property of the intelligentsia and the monied classes, serving their information needs

---

[33] Id. at 53-54.

[34] Maxwell E.P. King, *Journalism in an Egalitarian Society*, Sept. 1998 issue of Ethics in Journalism, publication of Washington and Lee's Department of Journalism and Mass Communication, pages 6-8.

and failing to meet the needs of the poorer communities." The focus on an elite readership, maintained King, helps explain why "newspaper companies are doing so well [financially] these days."

King's critique is echoed by Gregory Favre, vice president for news for the McClatchy Co. and by James Squires, former editor of Tribune Co.'s *Orlando Sentinel* and *Chicago Tribune*. Favre warns, "We cannot, as some have already done, restrict our circulation drives only to those areas of our cities that some advertisers want and many of our executives believe are the designated best areas of the cities."[35] Squires is confident that almost any circulation director, if given the resources–more copies, a lower price, promotion money–can boost circulation among less-affluent readers. "Why they are not employed," he observed, "is the dirty little secret of newspapering . . . . Because advertisers want only high-income, well-educated readers, publishers don't really want higher penetration in their market. . . . Thus, with few exceptions, the profitability of newspapers in monopoly markets has come to depend on an economic formula that is ethically bankrupt and embarrassing for a business that has always claimed to rest on public trust."[36]

Squires believes that a newspaper that follows his prescription to build inner-city circulation–added staff, coverage, ad sales, and promotion–would lose money doing that, "but you should do it," he contends, because newspapers are quasi-public institutions, which have to go in and deliver even if it costs money. It's not done, he said, because there's "no corporate ethic to serve the whole community."[37]

These observations are confirmed in reports and statements by spokesmen for the Newspaper Association of America, the organization of newspaper publishers. A 1995 NAA report purported

---

[35] Gregory Favre, *We Cannot Rest*, The Hayes Press-Enterprise Lecture Series, Number 34, April 5, 1999.

[36] James D. Squires, Read All About It! The Corporate Takeover of America's Newspapers, 1993 (Times Books) pages 88-91.

[37] Interview with Squires.

to show how reduced circulation makes economic sense.[38] "Good business decisions," it explained, "are not always volume-driven. One of the newspaper's most basic and fundamental principles is changing. That is, more is not necessarily better; better is better." The report's recommended strategies made it plain that "better" meant those readers who did not have to be lured by discounts, who could afford more "aggressive" prices, and who did not live in "fringe" areas. NAA's chief economist explained that "fringe circulation," which the report said should be eliminated, referred not just to readers far-removed geographically from advertisers but to readers with lower demographics. "Low-income areas," he said, "are not where you concentrate [circulation] efforts."[39]

Cathleen Black, then president and CEO of NAA, expressed the prevailing view of the organization in the mid-90's when she described the silver lining she saw in lost circulation: "While audited numbers continue to show circulation declines at many daily newspapers, much of it is due to internal business decisions newspapers are making, adjusting to changing market fundamentals. The result is that readership is up, or still very strong with key demographic groups, as newspapers respond to changing lifestyles by forging a stronger product and reader fit."

Stripped of euphemisms, her comments substantiate that the neglect of lower-income readers decried by King, Favre and Squires was part of a deliberate industry strategy to pursue a more upscale readership. In their 1997 book, "The Newspaper Publishing Industry," Robert G. Picard and Jeffrey H. Brody put the overall picture this way: "The practice of cutting circulation has increased in the past two decades, with papers halting circulation to areas where readers don't interest advertisers–such as inner cities or districts with lower incomes or other unwanted demographics–or where distribution costs are higher. Although these practices may serve the interests of the economic role of newspapers, they are harmful to newspapers' social

---

[38] 1995 Circulation Facts, Figures and Logic, Newspaper Association of America, p. 11.

[39] Interview with Miles E. Groves.

roles of conveying information and providing the communication links necessary for a healthy society."[40]

The authors added: "A few circulation studies related to chain-owned papers have been undertaken in recent years and have concluded that papers owned by newspaper groups tend to charge more for monthly subscriptions than independent newspapers. These results should not be surprising, because managers of chain-owned newspapers emphasize financial performance more than those at independent papers and place greater emphasis on pricing behavior."

Picard and Brody might have added that there are few incentives for newspaper company managers to stress circulation. Our examination of compensation committee reports of publicly traded newspaper companies shows that almost never is circulation a factor in CEO salary or bonus or stock-option awards. A notable exception: McClatchy, where performance on circulation is factored into all corporate bonuses. (It also accounts for at least 20 percent of publisher and editor bonuses.) CEO Gary Pruitt believes incentives tied to circulation explain in part why McClatchy is more successful than other companies in improving readership.

The importance of readership cannot be overstated. Newspapers are prime sources of in-depth news and information about public affairs, particularly about local issues. Newspaper readership is essential, therefore, for an informed electorate and an effectively functioning democracy. The long-term slide in circulation and readership means that newspapers are strangers in all too many households. Daily newspaper circulation dropped 34 percent between 1950 and 1995, from 356 per 1,000 population to 234 per 1,000; daily readership declined from 80.8 percent of the adult population in 1964 to 58.6 percent in 1998.

Moreover, more than a third of the editors we interviewed pointed to circulation as among the ways they measure their papers' quality. *Editor & Publisher*, the newspaper trade journal, agrees that

---

[40] Robert G. Picard and Jeffrey H. Brody, The Newspaper Publishing Industry (Boston: Allyn and Bacon, 1997) p. 89.

circulation "has a lot to do with the quality of the product."⁴¹ *Portland Oregonian* editor Sandra Mims Rowe echoes the sentiment when she says that the best way to tell whether newspapers have improved is if readership is up.⁴² If those who see a correlation between circulation and quality are correct, therefore, newspaper companies that fail to tie management compensation to circulation gains fail to heed a significant message being delivered about their papers by declining penetration numbers.

The drop in household penetration has multiple causes, many beyond the control of newspaper companies. But some measures they have taken, as noted above, have exacerbated the decline. Interviews with circulation directors at 90 of the largest U.S. dailies, by researchers at the University of Iowa's journalism school, made it evident that lower-income neighborhoods were being disadvantaged by such tactics as requiring payment in advance, refusing to deliver to public housing, door-to-door sales efforts only on days of the month when government checks were due, and denial of discounts. Combined with "aggressive pricing"–that is, charging more–the practices amount to writing off a whole class of potential readers. The growing resort to targeting or precision marketing has made it simpler, and even less expensive, to bypass the less affluent by aiming direct mail, telemarketing and door-to-door newspaper sales pitches at carefully selected targets. These targets tend to be "look-alikes," people with demographic characteristics similar to those of existing readers. They are also the demographic characteristics that appeal to advertisers, many of whom have made it clear that they much prefer a "desirable audience" to a large one. Newspaper "market books," the usually elaborate brochures newspapers use to impress advertisers, almost invariably boast about the higher education, professional status, home ownership and income of their readers. Lest the point be missed, a major 1998 ad by the newspaper industry in the *New York Times* declared in outsized

---

⁴¹ *Editorial*, Editor & Publisher, Aug. 21, 1999, p. 20.

⁴² Debra Gersh Hernandez, *Advice for the Future*, Editor & Publisher, Dec. 28, 1996, p. 11.

type, "Newspapers continue to supply reach and superior demographic targeting to advertisers that other local media cannot easily duplicate." The ad further emphasized in graphics how newspapers deliver "The Most Wanted Consumers."[43]

Are publicly traded newspapers, as a group, more likely than independents to neglect inner-city neighborhoods to secure upscale readership?[44] We do not have comprehensive data on the question. In theory, the unremitting bottom-line pressures on publicly traded companies from investors and analysts could cause them to be more prone than independents to downplay circulation efforts in low-income areas. A small-scale study we undertook supports such a hypothesis.

We broke down the circulation areas of four newspapers– *Detroit News* (Gannett), *Detroit Free Press* (Knight Ridder), *Baltimore Sun* (then Times Mirror) and *St. Petersburg Times* (independent)–by zip code, classified population in each zip code by race and income, and then examined newspaper penetration rates by zip code. Zip codes with a high proportion of blacks also were low income, and the lowest penetration was in areas with high concentrations of both low income and minority populations.

When zip codes with more than 50-percent black populations were compared, there were differences adjudged to be statistically significant between the performance of the *St. Petersburg Times* and the other papers. Whereas the *Times* registered respectable daily penetration rates of 44 percent and better in the high black areas, circulation in high-black areas in the other cities was markedly lower, with penetration rates most often in the teens. Single copies sell for

---

[43] Advertising Supp., *N.Y. Times*, Sept. 14, 1998.

[44] See, for example, James D. Squires, Read All About It!, p. 92: "Al Neuharth's parting words on his retirement [as Gannett chairman] in 1989 were that newspapers were still selling themselves too cheaply. They should be a dollar a copy, he advised, advocating the precise strategy he sold to Wall Street. Price maximizes revenue and holds down printing and distribution costs while cutting from the circulation base the unwanted low-income reader."

25 cents in St. Petersburg, 35 cents in Detroit and 50 cents in Baltimore. The *Times* is owned by an educational foundation, and its CEO, Andrew Barnes, said he worries if profits dip below 10 percent or exceed 20 percent. The Baltimore and Detroit papers are businesses owned by profit-maximizing companies whose stock prices are heavily influenced by earnings.

Does public ownership of newspapers create incentives for management to behave in the ways lamented by King, Favre and Squires: in effect, to cater to affluent suburbs and to turn their backs on inner cities? Generalizations are risky. Much depends on the outlook of management. Moreover, companies listed on stock exchanges aren't the only ones that strive for high profit margins. We found, for instance, that the *Milwaukee Journal*, employee-owned and with operating profit margins of about 20 percent, has circulation patterns in the inner city little different from Detroit and Baltimore. Nevertheless, if publicly traded newspaper companies are more prone to neglect low-income readers, that would be an exceedingly troubling downside of public ownership. Our limited survey points to the possibility that they are, and suggests the need for more data and further study.

Meanwhile, the newspaper industry may be having misgivings about its less-is-more approach to circulation. Mark Willes, then of Times Mirror, had wanted to expand readership of the *Los Angeles Times* by hundreds of thousands. The Newspaper Association of America has launched an $11.5 million campaign, headed by the marketer who helped double Coca-Cola's sales and stock price, to sell more newspapers. It is too soon to know, however, whether the industry intends by such measures to abandon, modify or intensify its "more is not better" philosophy, which increasingly has confined newspaper readership to an economic and social elite.

A related question is how much newspaper companies will be willing to cut into profits to build circulation. The industry spends relatively little on marketing. In the publicly traded sector of the industry, efforts to expand circulation by investing heavily in promotion can run smack into pressure to produce quarterly results to support the stock price.

D. The Shape of the Firm

Newspapers have traditionally been organized differently than the typical business firm. In many respects their organization has been intentionally inefficient, at least if efficiency is taken to mean profit maximization, expense minimization, and decisiveness. Their efficiency as firms providing news to the public, of course, is an entirely different matter.

The primary distinguishing hallmarks of a traditional newspaper company are (or until recently, were) threefold. First, the company is divided into two parts, business and news, each operating semi-autonomously from the other, but both focusing on the sale of the same product, the newspaper. The business part concerns itself with revenues, profits, selling advertisements, managing distribution, controlling the price of raw materials, developing and monitoring budgets, and the like. The news part is the editorial side, which concerns itself with gathering and processing information, determining what's important and what the reader wants in the newspaper, composing the news product, deciding what matters are of greatest importance, and rendering institutional views, or editorials, on a regular basis.

The business side of the newspaper is financially efficient, revenue driven, cost conscious, and oriented toward financial productivity in the way in which it performs its duties. The editorial side is sloppy, sometimes overstaffed, boisterous, usually consultative and deliberative, concerned about the quality of its news product as much as its cost. It is thus much like an academic institution: unruly, ungainly, individualistic, creative. Atop these two sides of the corporate personality sits the publisher, whose job it is to reconcile their competing demands and conceits. No self-respecting manufacturer of a mass-distributed consumer product would dare to organize itself this way.

The second distinguishing feature is that decision-making in a newspaper company is often slow and inclusive and even argumentative, governed not strictly by profit maximization, but instead by criteria of public importance, value, usefulness to the customers, truth, and the like. Profits are the concern of the publisher. News judgments are not shaped by revenue production or profit contribution or stock-market value.

The third feature concerns corporate purpose. The goal of the newspaper company is not simply wealth maximization of the owners and employees (not that they aren't interested in wealth or even profits). It is instead an ungainly combination of profit motive with public obligation and aspiration for public influence. These goals can be accommodated–balanced and traded off–but they cannot be made congruent. They do not reinforce each other, except in the sense of a dynamic tension. They always conflict. In that conflict, it might be claimed, lies the very heart of the journalistic adventure and, in its classic form, the soul of the newspaper enterprise in America.

Newspapers, then, can be said to imply certain organizational arrangements that depart from the norm for other industrial enterprises. In some measure, at least, these characteristics of inefficiency, cumbersomeness, and public mission can be viewed as definitional in character, hallmarks of organizations dedicated to providing the public with an independent source of information, interpretation, and opinion on matters judged important in a free society. This is not to say that changes in the organization of newspaper companies are by definition bad, compromising the ends of a free press. But it is to say that when changes occur, they should be assessed in terms of their impact on the important functions performed by newspaper companies.

The publicly traded newspaper company is changing many organizational features of the traditional newspaper company. Profit maximization is the principal objective of the publicly traded company and, increasingly, of its newspaper subsidiaries. The standards of efficiency implied by a profit-driven firm are being introduced into the news side of the company. Total circulation is less important than circulation's "quality," which often means its socio-economic and demographic composition. Target marketing and in some cases focusing of news content to specific markets are strategies employed to maximize advertising revenue, a richer potential source of income than subscriptions.

The two parts of the traditional newspaper company, news and business, are being brought together. The wall separating news from business, which was never impenetrable but was of symbolic importance and yielded practical consequences, is crumbling. The purpose served by the increasing interaction between, and occasional merger of, news and business is to more effectively align news decisions–staffing, editorial policy, general content–with the strictly financial standards of efficiency that pervade the rest of the organization. Some of this is being done from the top down, through the imposition of strict budget constraints that effectively circumscribe the autonomy that the news operations enjoy on matters of content, and through staffing and personnel policies, market research, and efficiency standards developed for news gathering, reporting, and processing in the firm. Some of it is coming from the bottom up, from preferences of the audience reflected through the highly focused lenses of segmentation and specialization of product, itself a reflection of advertiser demand for a more coherent and narrowly defined audience for their commercial messages.

But much of the realignment of news decisions along financial and profit-oriented lines is accomplished not with a stick, but with a carrot: large bonuses tied to revenues, expenses, and margins; stock-based awards tied to overall corporate performance and increased shareholder value that extend to editorial and news personnel. In subtle ways, these incentives may alter allegiances and sharpen the focus on financial consequences of news decisions. They can lead to financially-driven editorial decisions and to efforts, sometimes quite openly acknowledged, to "tear down" or disassemble the "wall" that protects the independence of editorial decisions from business decisions.[45]

---

[45] Many observers see the recent controversies about the Staples Center and the Office of Drug Policy as reflections of financially-driven editorial choices, and as resulting from breaches in the separation between news and business within the news organizations. The Staples Center controversy concerned a supplement in the *Los Angeles Times* that contained articles about the new Staples Center in Los Angeles, presented as editorial and news material, but actually published pursuant to a revenue-sharing and

In many important ways the publicly traded newspaper company now fits the organizational forms that are commonly used to describe the complex, diversified, and market-oriented industrial firms: profit-driven, hierarchical, marked by strict financial discipline imposed throughout the complex corporate organization, and compensation policies that strongly incentivize employees to maximize shareholder value. Similarly, the habits and organizational behaviors of complex diversified industrial companies are the very kinds of organizational structure and arrangements that typify a publicly traded, diversified, newspaper company. These behaviors include stock-market and short-term orientation; incentive systems tied strictly to financial performance measured largely by the financial markets; a parent company-subsidiary (newspaper) operating relationship that is decentralized as to product (news) and operational decisions, but highly centralized in terms of revenue, expense, and overall budget goals; use of objective (financial) standards of evaluation and compensation at the operating company (newspaper) level.

Such companies are described in the business and economic literature as unrelated diversified large firms: Large publicly traded

---

cooperative agreement between the paper and the Staples Center, an arrangement known by some members of the editorial staff but not by many of the reporters and not by the readers. Details of the incident can be found in the report prepared for the *Times* by David Shaw, published in the Times and available at *http://www.latimes.com.* and in William Prochnau, *Paradise Lost?*, Am. Journalism Review, Jan. 10, 2000. The Drug Policy controversy involved television networks and, it appears, newspapers around the country earning "credit" against the obligation to provide free advertising space for anti-drug ads by submitting independently published materials–editorial, news, and advertisements–that qualify for credit because they contain satisfactory anti-drug content, in the judgment of the federal government's Office of Drug Control Policy. See Howard Kurtz, *Drug Office Ad Deal Included Newspapers*, *Washington Post*, page C01, January 20, 2000.

companies that own many separate businesses, each of which is sufficiently distinct in product and customers that the operations cannot be consolidated but must be managed on a decentralized basis.[46] Newspaper holding companies fit this bill nicely: While each newspaper might appear, at first glance, to be the same, and thus the company may not seem to be too diversified in unrelated businesses, the fact is that the news (product) of each paper is distinct, and locally originated; the advertising base is largely distinct; the customers are distinct (differences from community to community, etc.).[47]

The management of such companies within a large organization is vested in a central executive organization, typically a holding company. The management of diverse operating companies requires, of necessity, delegation of substantial operating authority to the operating subsidiary companies. This is because no central manager can oversee the complex and diverse localized business

---

[46] For a sampling of the business and economics literature, see Calori & Cesma, *How Successful Companies Manage Diverse Businesses,* Long Range Planning, v. 21;3, pp 80-89 (1988); Collier, *Strategic Management in Diversified, Decentralized Companies*, Journal of Business Strategy, v. 3, pp. 85-89; Hall, *Reflections on Running a Diversified Company*, Harvard Business Review, v. 65, pp. 84-93 (1987); Hiskisson & Hitt, *Strategic Control Systems and Relative R&D Investment in Large Multiproduct Firms*, Strategic Management Journal, v.9, pp. 605-21 (1988); Kerr, *Strategies and Managerial Rewards: An Empirical Study*, Academy of Management Journal, v. 28, pp. 155-79 (1985); Russo, *Bureaucracy, Economic Regulation, and Incentive Limits of the Firm*, Strategic Management Journal, v. 103, pp. 103-118 (1992); Williamson, Markets and Hierarchies (1975); Dumaine and Labate, *Is Big Still Good?* Fortune, Apr. 20, 1992, p. 50.

[47] Some of the companies in our study are attempting to reduce the "unrelatedness" of the newspaper companies by standardizing portions of the news content or composition.

decisions that are often unique to each operating company. It is also because the central management of such companies (i.e. the CEO, the CFO, and other executive management) are typically not familiar with the nuances of the businesses that are owned. Managements are largely focused on the overall financial performance of the firm, its overall strategy, and the investment market in which its stockholders operate and to which it owes its principal obligation.

The management of large companies of this sort tends to be less familiar with, or involved in, the operations of the owned businesses, less concerned with the quality of those businesses, more committed to satisfying the higher profit expectations of the owners (stockholders), and more concerned with maximizing profit. When the large companies are publicly traded, the firms are subject to intense market scrutiny, management is subject directly to the expectations of the financial markets, short-term profit and returns become important focuses, and long-term planning at the level of the operating company (as opposed to longer term strategy at the level of the central firm, which acts much like an investment company with changing strategy based on general market and economic conditions) is not emphasized.

Short-term thinking dominates the operations of the subsidiary companies in the diversified public company, as do short-term financial targets and results. Tight budget, margin, and profit controls imposed on the operating company by the parent leave the operating company much apparent, or formal, autonomy but little capacity to exercise it, make longer-term planning and investment in such things as quality of product difficult if not impossible to carry out at the operating company (newspaper) level. Strategy at the top corporate level is market driven, but not in terms of the market of customers at the operating newspaper level. At the corporate level, the primary customer is the stockholder, and the product to be delivered is the return on the stockholder's investment.

As a result, a primary concern of top management is to govern the subsidiaries in a way that maximizes shareholder wealth. Corporate management accomplishes this by controlling capital and resource allocation among subsidiaries; by following a general portfolio strategy by which the corporation plans according to the expected results of the individual subsidiary strategies; centralizes the overall strategic control at the head corporate office (while delegating operating responsibilities to the subsidiaries), and centralizes overall financial control and resource allocation at the head office.[48]

Diversified corporations are more risk-averse and focus more on short-term efficiency and profits than do their independent counterparts. Consistent with this, the judgment of managerial performance tends to be more objective in diversified firms, as compared to the largely subjective evaluation in single-business firms. This is because top management lacks specific business knowledge about the operations and business of the subsidiaries, and therefore personalized and subjective evaluation (which rests on such knowledge) is simply not feasible in a large, diversified firm. Top corporate management's pervasive reliance upon financial indicators to evaluate subsidiary management performance–enhanced, in our study, by "carrots" of stock options reinforcing the same financial criteria–may lead subsidiary managers (publishers and editors) to be even more concerned with financial performance than managers of an independent company. If this is the case, then (notwithstanding nominal autonomy in operations) subsidiary managers may have less discretion to act in a way that does not, above all else, maximize shareholder wealth.

This general description of the organization and management behavior of publicly traded diversified firms mirrors the organizational arrangements and practices that we have outlined in the previous sections for the publicly traded newspaper companies. In these large consolidated firms, newspaper companies no longer enjoy unique organizational attributes and special patterns of decision making and behavior explainable largely by the public mission of an independent newspaper. Instead, they have come increasingly to look like any other large and diversified manufacturer and distributor of a consumer product.

---

[48] Hiskisson & Hitt, *Strategic Control Systems and Relative R&D Investment in Large Multiproduct Firms*, Strategic Management Journal, v.9, pp. 605-21 (1988).

As discussed at length in the preceding sections, the boards of directors and central executive management of the publicly traded newspaper firms are strongly oriented to the financial markets and to increasing shareholder values. This focus places a premium on short-term operating results, especially in the subsidiary operating companies, the newspapers. The operating companies are managed much like an investment portfolio, not like the heart of the parent company's business operations. Properties can be bought and sold much like securities. And they are.

Controls on the operating newspapers are highly centralized for financial matters, and decentralized on editorial matters. But financial controls on budgets, personnel, and revenues place sharp constraints on the newspapers' capacity to exercise their nominal editorial freedoms. Standards of evaluation and compensation are almost exclusively objective, and largely, if not entirely, based on financial targets. Compensation for managers of the newspapers is based in substantial (often very substantial) part on bonuses geared to achieving or exceeding financial budget targets. Incentive compensation at the newspaper-company level typically takes the form of stock, in the form either of stock awards or stock options, in combination with bonuses tied to financial targets for the operating newspaper. The operating companies are thus given strong incentives to accomplish the shareholder-value objectives of the overall firm. The operating management and key editorial and news personnel are made stockholders, and thus shareholder-wealth objectives may become their own personal objectives, as well. In these and other respects discussed earlier, the newspaper company is being gradually and often subtly transformed in its formal organization and in its business behavior.

Two interrelated forces appear to explain much if not all of this transformation. The first is the public financial markets and the incentives and requirements they impose. The financial markets (the stock market), as discussed in detail in earlier sections, represent return-maximizing institutional and individual investors. These are passive investors in a market designed efficiently to determine value in the entire range of publicly traded companies. The common standard of value is profit, return on investment, and increased shareholder value as reflected in the market price of the company's stock. The market is, perhaps by competitive necessity, largely product- and business-neutral (or indifferent); short-term in its orientation and valuation, as the investments available there (whether in GM or Gannett stock) are highly liquid, capable of being shifted at a moment's notice. The market's short-term and strictly investment-based expectations drive any public company to adopt the market standards for itself, for the company does not exist independently of the market. It is owned by it.

The second force accounting for the transformation of the publicly traded newspaper company is the nature of the firm itself–a large firm with distinct or operationally unrelated subsidiaries–and the resultant organizational form that in many ways is necessary for management of such a business. That is, even without the publicly traded stock, some of what we find in the operation and incentive structure of the diversified newspaper firms would still exist (though perhaps less pervasively in consolidated newspaper companies). The exertion of substantial management control and discipline over diversified activities requires standardization, clear and direct objectives, hierarchy and minimum bureaucracy (subjective standards would require elaborate procedures and bureaucracy), and positive incentives for compliance with overall corporate goals.

There is, however, a third force, a feature of the newspaper company and the news business that distinguishes it from most other companies, such as General Motors, for example. The newspaper company has two inherently competing markets or constituencies: the readers, who want and need the news; and the advertisers, who want the news delivered in a package that will make their commercial messages most effective. General Motors serves those who purchase their cars: their corporate organization, efficiency, even short-term orientation is ultimately determined by the actions of the customers. If a newspaper company were like GM, the newspaper company's behavior and profit orientation would be judged by whether the readers chose to buy, or to continue buying, the company's product.

But because advertisers today contribute about 80 percent of newspaper revenues, by far the strongest customers of newspapers are the advertisers and the readers the advertisers wish to reach, not the broader subscriber or circulation market. Efficiency in the newspaper firm, in other words, has not just altered the way in which the companies respond to their customer base, it has instead shifted the dominant customer base for corporate and financial purposes, from the public audience for news to the advertisers, who use the newspaper as an instrument for distribution of commerce. The newspaper company is thus being doubly transformed by the markets and by the changing shape of the firm.

To the extent that both external market forces and implicit management necessity are contributing to the transformation of the publicly traded newspaper organization, any attempt to blunt or alter the undesirable consequences of the organizational changes must address not only the financial market forces, but also relevant aspects of the corporate structure and the firms' organizational behavior.

E. The New Newspaper Enterprise

Corporations are vehicles for profit-driven commercial activity. This has always been so. Why, then, have newspaper corporations experienced such dramatic changes in organization, form, and orientation over the past 15 or so years? There are a number of possible answers.

The first answer is that newspaper corporations have undergone no radical change at all. The skin of the enterprise, now marked by horizontal combinations in newspaper holding companies, may have changed, but what is beneath it hasn't. Historically there is no reason to conclude that earlier newspapers (at the turn of the 19th Century or in the mid 20th) were any less profit-driven and governed by self-interest. One need think only of the Hearst and Pulitzer papers, which were known for debased content and large combinations into chains. The scale of papers in the early 20th century was smaller, even in the metropolitan areas, but not much so. And competition existed in most markets, as it does not (at least in the newspaper market as opposed to the communication market) today. Competition surely constrained newspaper content, and may have maintained some measure of quality in the product.

Technology, however, has changed, and with substantial consequences. The changed economies of scale have permitted publications to scale down, to focus on narrower markets, and to do so profitably. Newspaper content, as a consequence, has become more adapted to specific audiences and demographic groups. This means that news, the substance of the business, is becoming varied, less fungible. Instead of a market in which more than one company vied for customers by doing a different or better job of reporting the same events, the market is changing to one in which various newspapers compete less with each other, but instead focus on their segments of a market, and in turn spend less time on reporting on the common events that we might call news, focusing instead on different events and stories and issues that are specific to their audiences. Competition, in other words, is changing from competition with other newspapers, to competition to find the audience's preferences and tastes – competition for, and thus with, the audience.

As news is becoming less uniform, as the meaning of news is beginning to break down, the allegiance of the newspaper companies to their product is also breaking down, with the result that the product, news, is becoming just another market-based commodity to be altered to fit tastes, and to be marketed in a way that is profit-maximizing. Newspaper companies used to be companies built up around the news and its distribution. They were companies with a mission–a public mission and a private one, too–governed by their product, which had a certain degree of fixed content, meaning, and relevance and importance. Newspaper companies today are more akin to financial enterprises dedicated to profit and market value, with "newspaper" a product of chimerical quality to be changed and shaped, bought or sold off, as the demands of commerce dictate. As newspaper companies have lost allegiance to "the newspaper" and "the news," news has begun to take on the quality of a commodity without intrinsic importance or fixed content.

But even though the market has changed and thus the allegiance to the product of news is changing, has the profit imperative and market-driven character of the enterprise changed? Fundamentally, the profit motive of the newspaper company has not changed. But a few surrounding forces have. First, when newspapers were owned by a family or a few local business people, and run by a secure management over the long haul, profit seems to have been less imperative–or at least the size of the profit was less imperative. This may partly be due to the fact that, for the newspaper owner of old, profit was taken partly in the form of power and prestige. In many ways these alternative motivating forces were no better for the newspaper, as owner ideology and influence often shaped the news, and the newspaper's allegiance to the power structure of the community may have been too great. Profit could also be taken, in part, in the form of a stable of famous and celebrated writers, associations that increased the social and intellectual standing of the owners.

Second, the dominating and unrelenting expectations of the national investment markets are now being felt directly by newspapers. In the late 20th century the financial markets expanded rapidly, making capital easily available to larger and successful enterprises; indeed, demanding more and more opportunities for capital investment as the quantity of savings increased throughout the society. For the newspaper business, the bargain struck was a Faustian one: capital was available for the newspaper industry, but with it came a new set of expectations. An investing market demanded returns on its investment, for newspaper investments were fungible with all other forms of enterprise, and money would gravitate to those investments best able to thrive in a *pure* financial market. The newspaper companies found that the economies of scale combined with new technologies for printing and distribution of news made newspapers highly profitable financial commodities. Newspapers were engines of untapped potential advertising revenue, unkempt and sloppily-run operations ripe for the cost-cutter's picking, enterprises whose product, hard news, could be stripped and made efficient because the product in its traditional form bore no relation to the news imperatives of focused audiences and premium advertising rates.

This was not like General Motors, with external market forces requiring GM to make better cars more efficiently in order to increase revenues and profits. It was instead as if the markets told GM to forget about the kind of cars it makes, and instead use them only as instruments for accomplishing other ends. Newspapers were encouraged, in other words, to see news simply as the engine for, or instrument of, delivering eyeballs for advertising, because the advertisers paid most of the bill anyway. News could be stripped, made efficient, reshaped without concern about content or quality or public purpose, as long as the new news product could attract the desirable advertising market or audience. Advertisers generally don't care about the public side of news or about news quality. Most simply care about reaching an audience efficiently, which is to say as cheaply as possible, and with maximum yield for the product being advertised. Advertisers became a prime constituency of newspaper companies, and quality of circulation became more important than quantity.

The new newspaper that took shape around this paradigm formed holdings of many newspapers, standardized them financially, allowed them to adapt to their market or market segment, and sold the resulting financial machine to the investing public. Being now bound by the market's bargain, the energies of the newspaper companies shifted from the news product, its quality, and the public value of the news business, to the growth in revenue, return on equity, and stock value that could be produced in ever greater quantities by the business of news. The companies became pure financial enterprises, incentivized by pure financial-market standards of performance. For stockholders who were investors with little interest in the news business, but interested only in their investment returns, either the news business would have to change or they would simply shift their funds to another product–telephones, computers, cars, steel, or anything else.

This form of financial- and market-oriented concern would logically move in a few clear directions. First, financial controls–revenues, expenses, yields, budgets–would be centralized in the parent company, for that company is the one owned by and obedient to the market. Second, the goals of the parent company would be reoriented to financial-market performance. Compensation would be calibrated to stock prices and profits. Top management would be given options and bonuses geared largely if not exclusively to short- and medium-term investment performance. For top management of the holding company–in reality an investment company–the job qualifications would not necessarily be news experience, but financial acumen, financial systems, operations controls, marketing, efficiency. These would be the young MBAs, persons drawn from the investment-banking community, chief executives drawn from other consumer industries: industries such as food, disposable items, retail sales, advertising and marketing, whose nature was similar to the nature of the new business of news–indeed for all practical financial purposes, those industries were indistinguishable.[49]

The operating newspapers, the subsidiaries, were another matter altogether. They would be severed off from the parent, abstracted from the holding company's business, at least in terms of the substantive content of what they published. The owners, millions of them (represented by a few institutional investors), were no longer interested in substituting pride and social station for profit, and cared little about the product of the newspaper unless, of course, it failed to yield to the central management's financial discipline and profit demands. Operating margins for the newspapers were set at ever-increasing heights, climbing from historic rates of 8 or 10 percent to 15 percent, then to 20, then to 25, then to 30 percent (and even, in a few cases, higher).

The public companies often first operated in markets already decimated by the tough economics of traditional news, where subscription revenues were critical and audience was declining; competition, in other words, had already been driven out in the precipitous 20-year decline in the number of daily newspapers in the United States. But the companies didn't necessarily act like monopolists by hiking subscription prices. Subscription revenues would become a smaller, even incidental, piece of the revenue pie in their long term strategies. Instead, they acted like monopolists by

---

[49] As Leo Bogart, an authority on the press with long experience in the Newspaper Advertising Bureau, observed in the Spring/Summer 1999 Media Studies Journal, "Publicly held newspaper corporations are run increasingly by professional managers rather than by individuals steeped in the tradition of public-service journalism."

cutting their cost structure, *and often the news associated with it*; they shed unwanted circulation, discounted subscription prices and target-marketed to get and keep the most desirable (socioeconomically) circulation; they invested in sophisticated production and distribution technology that enabled them to produce a better and more focused advertising vehicle and to adapt its content–news and advertisements –to different segments of its audiences, producing many newspapers where there had been only one, through zoning and packaging; and then they increased the amount of advertising and hiked the advertising rates. These new companies saw themselves and sold themselves as a uniquely efficient medium for advertising. To the extent that competition was not a factor for the operating newspapers –they owned their communities or their market niches, and therefore could command high prices from their advertisers who supplied the revenues–there was no reason to worry about the terms of competition (at least with other newspapers), for competition didn't exist. There was no reason, in other words, to worry about quality, scope of news coverage, indeed even the professional experience of the news reporters. The operating companies, in short, didn't need to be incentivized in the same way as the holding companies. Relatively cheap labor could be hired, staffing cut and productivity could be increased, standardization could be used as a substitute for experience and substantive quality.

Incentives were needed at the newspaper level only as a means of assuring the allegiance of the local management–publisher, advertising executive and, often, the editor, whose duty it was to wield the ax and enforce the discipline of efficiency in the remaining newsroom. These people tended, in any event, to be "company" people, not community people; sometimes they were even formally made employees of the parent company, not the operating newspaper company that they managed. They were intent on moving up through the ranks of the parent company over time, and so they needed little else by way of incentive: modest stock options, perhaps, to give them a stake in the financial market's valuation of what they were doing. But they needed a kind of "stick," which almost always took the form of compensation based partly on fixed salary and partly–a significant part, usually–on a formula-based bonus linked to on meeting or exceeding budget targets.

This picture of the new newspaper enterprise is a grim one, at least for those persons who are dedicated to the public mission of daily news. But having painted such a picture, it must also be said that the newspaper business didn't change itself. This isn't a story about avaricious bad people having gotten too much power and having debased an industry purely for personal gain. The newspaper industry was instead changed largely by external technological, economic, and market forces. Newspapers in the older sense of the term–local, family-owned, driven by public purpose or ideology, not driven by market performance or maximum profitability–didn't change. They just died off, to be replaced by new content injected into the old skin.

This suggests one of two conclusions: (1) accept the fact of change as imperative and unchangeable, the dictate of the invisible hand, and don't try hopelessly and futilely to change people, habits, and values in the newspapers of today; or (2) seek change at the structural level, through modification of the organization and incentives that characterize the corporate institution and market-based form of today's newspaper business. We will suggest a number of possible reforms in Chapter VI.

Chapter V

The Changed Economic and Competitive Environment: Technology and the New Economics of News[50]

The deep structural changes that have occurred in the newspaper industry are not the products of chance or will. They are largely the consequences of economic and technological change. The role of technology and economic forces in shaping news and news organizations is not newly discovered. Observing the trends in 1947 toward monopolization, centralization of economic and media power in the hands of only a few, large mass media news outlets, and the influence of advertisers on news content, the *Hutchins Commission*[51] called on the press to exercise its high civic and social responsibility, to seek truth and accuracy and perspective, to afford opportunity for diverse voices to be heard, to afford readers and listeners real choice. The report's conclusions and recommendations were largely shaped by the commission's assessment of the economics of journalism and news at mid-century. Today the economics of journalism have radically changed.

---

[50] Much of the material in this section is drawn from a much longer article written by Randall Bezanson on the role of economics and technology in shaping news, editorial judgment, and journalism. Randall Bezanson, *The Atomization of the Newspaper: Technology, Economics and the Coming Transformation of Editorial Judgments About News,* 3 Commun. Law & Policy 175-230 (1998).

[51] The Commission on Freedom of the Press, A Free and Responsible Press: A General Report on Mass Communication: Newspapers, Radio, Motion Pictures, Magazines, and Books (Robert D. Leigh, ed. 1947) [hereinafter the *Hutchins Commission Report*].

Much of the change in the newspaper business is the product of underlying technological and economic forces, just as the vision of a free press the Hutchins Commission sought to recapture in its famous 1947 report, *A Free and Responsible Press*, had been a product of economic forces. What are these forces and how have they shaped the American institution of a free press and its engine, editorial judgment; what new combination of forces led to the Hutchins Commission's concerns about the press' change in mid-century; and, most important, what forces today are creating further change?

A. Economics and the Emergence of the Newspaper

The basic force that accounted for the rise in press freedom and the emergence of editorial judgment in the 18th and 19th centuries was technology. The force that led to increased concentration and monopoly power in the news business in the early 20th century was technology. And the force that is leading now to dramatic changes in the news industry is technology. These changes have led to an implosion of the mass audience and the emergence of fragmentation and market specialization, to the great influence of advertisers and audiences on "news," to the rise of entertainment values in news, and ultimately, perhaps, to the radical transformation of news and journalism, and the forms of editorial judgment that distinguish them.

Editorial judgment is largely a product of what is possible (technology) and therefore what is profitable (economics).[52] The

---

[52] Editorial judgment is the foundation upon which all of journalism is built. But the foundation is hidden from view. It is remarkable how little journalists, and even academics in the field of journalism, have to say about editorial judgment. In texts it is discussed in terms of skills: filling newsholes; qualities of immediacy, interest, and the position and role of editor, etc. Communications scholars spend a great deal of time trying to dissect

V / Technology and the New Economics of News / 117

technology of printing made it *possible* to reach large audiences. With the rise of economic freedom and increasingly dispersed individual wealth in 17th- and 18th-century England, using the technology to reach large audiences became *profitable*. The metropolitan dailies in London, which began as expensive publications for the elite and politically connected, were transformed into more democratic institutions serving larger and increasingly

---

and parse editorial judgment, hoping to capture through what has been done, what is and should be done. See Pamela Shoemaker and Stephen D. Reese, Mediating the Message (2nd ed. 1996). Gatekeeping studies abound. Philosophers and political theorists refer to editorial judgment, though most often in passing. See J. Herbert Altschull, From Milton to McLuhan, The Ideas Behind American Journalism (1990); Alvin W. Gouldner, The Dialectic of Ideology and Technology (1976). And First Amendment types, in law and in journalism and, now, in the communications media, regularly genuflect to it. Even the Supreme Court pays obeisance with such adoring but unhelpful phrases as "editing is what editors are for." CBS v. Demo. Nat'l Comm., 412 U.S. 94, 124-25 (1973); Miami Herald Pub. Co. v. Tornillo, 418 U.S. 241 (1974).

But surprisingly few have attempted to give the foundational concept any content. Whatever its specifics, editorial judgment as applied to news (another widely spoken but rarely explored term) is the only basis upon which journalists can distinguish themselves from comedians, fiction writers, purveyors of obscenity, or proselytizers of religion or politics.

The press, it seems, has always been caught in a magnetic tug of war between the demand of the audience and the demand of its trade, journalism; between its base instincts and its better judgment. The constant tension is necessary. The threat today is that the tension will dissipate–that the audience demands and the baser instincts will prevail too much.

diverse audiences.[53] Fast on their heels came the provincial weeklies and dailies that drew upon the metropolitan papers for content and mastered the technological art of economical–by which is meant cheap–newspaper production.[54]

For these new outlets of information a mechanism was needed by which information could be gathered, the universe of possible subjects and objects of publication could be screened, and the resulting choices shaped into a publication that would serve the interests of its purchasers. In an environment of increasing political freedom and economic individualism, much demand existed for access to current information on "politics and political economy," as it would be described in 1849 by the People's Charter Union,[55] a group that was actively involved in the struggle against the Stamp Act in 18th- and 19th-century England. The mechanism for selecting material to be published for this rapidly increasing audience was what we now think of as editorial judgment, or news judgment. Its criteria were perfectly understandable given the conditions at the time: independence from government (which had previously controlled what political and economic information people received); gathering and selection of specific information from a large body of facts and events; a concentration on current information on political and economic subjects affecting peoples' lives in very specific ways; packaged in a form that was (a) cheap, (b) accessible, and (c) that would give the reader the power to select what he or she wanted to

---

[53] Frederick S. Seibert, Freedom of the Press in England, 1476-1776 (1952) ; Randall P. Bezanson, Taxes on Knowledge in America: Exactions on the Press from Colonial Times to the Present (1994).

[54] Id.

[55] Collet Dobson Collet, History of the Taxes on Knowledge: Their Origin and Repeal, 42-46 (facs. repr. 1971) (1933); *see* Randall P. Bezanson, Taxes on Knowledge in America (1994).

read, and which would be presented in a way that made its reading enjoyable.[56]

The technology of printing and mass production on a scale that brought costs way down made this possible. Without the technology, the underlying economic and social forces would have been stillborn, as they had been in England for at least the previous 200 years. It was technology that shaped the way in which these underlying social and economic forces became manifest, and it was technology that therefore shaped what we think of as "news," what we now enshrine as editorial judgment, and what we have come to know as a "newspaper."

When transplanted to America in the 18th and 19th centuries, the technology evolved, and the ideas of "news" and editorial judgment were refined and extended, but not fundamentally altered.[57] With the increasing urbanization that came with the industrial revolution and the growth of large cities, the audience for news grew

---

[56] "The journalist . . . has a positive duty to serve as a realist, not an ideologue, to seek out the true facts so that they might be used to help organize and preserve, as [Alexander] Bickel wrote, 'decent, wise, just, responsive, stable government in the circumstances of a given time and place.'" Altschull at 131, quoting Alexander Bickel, *Reconsideration: Edmund Burke*, New Republic, March 17, 1973, at 34.

[57] While the press in the early American period was often licentious, an inclination that gave rise to the "responsible for abuses" language of the state constitutions, the struggles over press freedom, marked most vividly by the Zenger case and the Croswell case, involved the press' freedom to publish information about persons that was damaging but true, or published in a good-faith belief about truth. That is, the material was published pursuant to a judgment that the information was important for people to have, as it pertained to public men and measures, and was true. See generally, Anderson, *The Origins of the Press Clause*, 30 U.C.L.A. L.Rev. 455 (1983); Leonard Levy, Legacy of Suppression (1960).

almost exponentially.[58] This made possible the emergence of the penny press and with it the large and comprehensive press institutions: the companies that sought the news, sorted it, printed it, and distributed it under one roof and on a scale that permitted very low costs per unit.[59] The product, the newspaper, was made even cheaper by the growth of advertising by merchants seeking efficient access to the mass market, companies striving for a metropolitan, regional, state, and even national market. The job of editorial judgment was focused increasingly on reflecting the tastes of ever larger audiences with varying interests (urban, rural), incorporating them into the news screen, and synthesizing them into a single information product that would be written to catch the attention and allegiance of the larger and more diverse market. Thus the skill of infusing style and entertainment into the presentation of news, a skill present from the very first metropolitan daily because it was inherent in the reach of the print technology, was honed to a fine art by the Pulitzers, Hearsts, and others.[60]

This new and expanding market served by the penny press was a market of increasing homogeneity: increasingly urban; increasingly wealthy; increasingly involved in industrialization and the resulting work experiences and social and economic conditions. Were this not so, the rise of the large and consolidated news company would not have been possible. It was this growing and homogeneous market that made economies of scale profitable, and for which technological development was driven. The mass market fostered the trend toward concentration on a national, regional, and local level, a

---

[58] See Michael Schudson, Discovering the News: A Social History of American Newspapers (1978); Bezanson, Taxes on Knowledge in America (1994); Mitchell Stephens, A History of News (1988).

[59] Schudson, *supra* note 58.

[60] See Herbert Altschull, From Milton to McLuhan, The Ideas Behind American Journalism (1990) ; Schudson, *supra* note 58.

trend that troubled the Hutchins Commission.[61] The possibility that the decisions about news–the exercise of editorial judgment–would rest in too few hands, and that those hands would be so driven by personal ideology or by economic forces that news would be debased, driven out by entertainment and gossip and self-interest, became the commission's rallying cry.[62]

These matters, of course, presented serious problems and were legitimate subjects for concern. Economic forces could clearly debase editorial judgment. But they could not transform it or eliminate it, for large mass audiences served by increasingly large firms depended on the work of editorial judgment, filtering that which people want and need, and putting it in a form that will make the mass audience want it. The work of editorial judgment, in other words, was to present information profitably, by which is meant attractively, to a huge and still diverse group of subscribers. Large scale made editorial judgment more important, not less; indeed, it fostered the emergence of journalism as an academic discipline, as a "profession," and it caused "editorial judgment" to be reduced to common elements and processes that could be effectively standardized for the large firm.[63] This was the heyday of editorial judgment and journalism.

---

[61] *Hutchins Commission Report* 1-20.

[62] *Id.* at 52-54.

[63] Schudson, supra note 58. Herbert Altschull describes a study by Mark Fishman, who "found in his examination of a California newspaper that a set of professional practices and routines gives news organizations a uniform view of the world that is, in our sense, ideological (i.e., not philosophy but practical ends). The professional ideology of journalists takes its shape from how reporters and editors understand the philosophical ideas that are fundamental in the American culture." Altschull, *supra* note 52, at 17, citing Mark Fishman, Manufacturing the News 134-140 (1980).

B. Changing Economic and Technological Forces at Mid-Century

But by the time the Hutchins Commission issued its 1947 Report decrying the conditions of the press–its larger and larger scale, its increased concentration, its debasement of taste and focus on entertainment, and its fascination with the peculiar rather than the important [64] –the tides had already turned, the apex had been reached and the new challenge would not be solving the old problems but discovering the new ones. And it was not in economic forces, as such, that the new problems would be found, but in technology, though to be sure, economic forces had much to do with the emergence of the new technology.

New underlying economic and social forces were at work even in 1947: Increased personal wealth, widely dispersed; changing patterns of work and living; the development of the suburbs, centers of cultural and political and economic differences within a previously monolithic and dehumanizing urban environment; increasing access to education by the working classes.[65] The monolithic industrial and urban experiences of the mass audience were breaking down.

But the critical development in the field of news would be technological. And the technological change would be revolutionary. Technology would enable the economies of production to be shifted, indeed reversed, from the large scale to the small scale; it would remove barriers to entry; it would alter the economic paradigm, making it more profitable to narrow and focus an audience than to broaden and expand it. Technology would generate greatly increased competition, which would serve in part as a means of giving the smaller audiences greater definition. It would make publication on a small scale inexpensive and efficient. It would afford advertisers seeking customers the chance to focus their messages in a narrower

---

[64] *Hutchins Commission Report* at 54-57.

[65] See Schudson, *supra* note 58; Randall Bezanson, *The Right to Privacy Revisited: Privacy, News, and Social Change, 1890-1990*, 80 Calif. L. Rev. 1133 (1992).

medium, shedding emphasis on the mass market and reaching the target market for which advertisers would pay much more per person reached. It would shift emphasis in publication decisions toward audience desire, which would now be focused not on general matters of taste and preference but, with a narrower and more demographically homogeneous audience, toward issues of specific interest. The newspaper market, in short, would move from wholesale toward retail, and with it editorial judgment about news would become increasingly audience-bounded.

The technology, of course, was telecommunications (the capacity to communicate vast amounts of information cheaply and quickly to any location), the computer (the ability to generate text and image, shape it and alter it easily and without cost, and to move it directly to production without the steps of typesetting), and new printing, production, and distribution technologies (laser technology, satellite printing, information collection and management). These technological developments have resulted in the breakup of the mass audience as publication on a small scale has become possible, efficient, and economically attractive. Small-scale publication has enabled the breakup of the dominant firm that was once possessed of monopoly power over news and information in a market; the emergence of greater inter-media competition for news, and greater competition in the print (newspaper) industry from small and specialized publications; the breaking apart into separate and specialized firms of the news acquisition, selection, production, and distribution stages once maintained under one roof; the breakup of the news organizations' monopoly on access to and possession of information;[66] the growth of new companies specializing in particular stages of the previously unified news process (data-base companies, news-gathering companies, printing companies, distribution

---

[66] This, of course, is largely a product of information technology, data-base technology, and low-cost communication mediums like the Internet, through which freestanding companies have emerged for the specialized purpose of storing and reselling information, and the capacity to obtain and use that information has been made inexpensive and universally available to the individual.

companies); and, perhaps most important for our purposes, increasing participation by the audience in editorial judgment about news.[67]

The Hutchins Commission couldn't, of course, see into the future. These dramatic changes were only beginning to take shape in 1947. But they make much of the report irrelevant today–technologically anachronistic is perhaps the best phrase. The report's articulation of the general concerns and aims of a free press are not entirely irrelevant, but the causes of their jeopardy are. And even some aspects of the general concern about responsibility and the general ends of a free press are of doubtful pertinence today. Radical changes in technology and economic forces in the news industry, and particularly the daily newspaper industry, require serious rethinking about the very content of the idea of a free press and free editorial judgment. The newspaper organization is fundamentally changing because of technology, and the very idea of editorial judgment is in the midst of a radical shift from the news organization to the reader, altering our very understanding of what news is and how it must be understood to occur.[68]

---

[67] See Chapter IV section C; Chapter V section C.

[68] Robert MacNeil, in a speech entitled "More News, Lower Standards," put it in the following way: "If people begin to choose news items for themselves from the vast cafeteria on the Internet, in effect making their own newspaper or news broadcast, it will mean an enormous loss of editorial authority and power in the institutions that currently [produce] newspapers and broadcasts." *http://www.freedomforum.org/FreedomForum/resources/media_ and_soc/tech_future/macneilspch.html.*

C. The New Economic Imperatives of News: The Atomization of News and the Newspaper

"The future belongs to neither the conduit or content players, but to those who control the filtering, searching, and sense-making tools we will rely on to navigate through the expanse of cyberspace."[69]

In the 19th century, Neil Postman has said, journalism was based on the scarcity of information. Today and in the future, journalism will be based on the oversupply of information. "The problem is how to decide what is significant, relevant information, how to get rid of the unwanted information."[70]

Will the journalist keep a foothold in the information-sorting and selecting task of the future, providing those qualities of selflessness, honesty, public need, and perspective that editorial judgment came to mean with the rise of the mass media of news in the 19th century? Or will technology so unbundle[71] and segment the journalist's market that the task of gathering and assembling will be all that remains for journalism in an institutional setting (which is to say journalism with a semblance of standardization, professionalism, and thus reliability)? The more substantive tasks of sorting and filtering and distributing will be shifted elsewhere, perhaps to software filters, and ultimately to each of us as consumers enabled to impose our own interests and preferences and prejudices–our own unique bundling– on the news we choose to receive.[72]

---

[69] Paul Saffo, of the Institute for the Future, quoted in Katherine Fulton, *A Tour of Our Uncertain Future*, Colum. Journ. Review, March-April 1996.

[70] Neil Postman, quoted in Katherine Fulton, *A Tour of Our Uncertain Future, supra* note 69.

[71] Katherine Fulton, *supra* note 69.

[72] Katherine Fulton surveys some of the ways in which individual preferences and tastes can be used as filters on the Web

Perhaps the major premise of the *Hutchins Commission Report* was that ownership of the outlets for mass communication was becoming too concentrated. The report criticized the concentration of the press in only a few very large institutions, and noted that economies of scale, with increasing amounts of information to be captured and reported, favored largeness at the expense of competition and diversity.[73] Concentration was leading, as Lee Bollinger put it, to "a drastic constriction in the base of the funnel of information and ideas, so great as to cast into doubt the continued viability of the principle that truth will more likely emerge from the conflicting expressions in the marketplace."[74]

---

today, in *A Tour of Our Uncertain Future, supra* note 69. "These experiments," she writes, "begin to hint at the really radical thing about new technologies: they enable people to have more control over what they want to know and when they want to know it. . . ." The much-touted personal newspaper [produced by experimental software developed at MIT], which allows people to adjust for their own combinations of news, opinion, and features, is already offered by a college student (CRAYON), a major new entrepreneurial effort (Individual, Inc.), and the San Jose Mercury News (Newshound). Id.

For an academic introduction to one form of this segmented and even individuated selection technology, see Michael Resnick, *Distributed Constructionism*, published in Proceedings of the International Conference on the Learning Sciences, Association for the Advancement of Computing in Education, Northwestern University (July 1996). With specific reference to community-based selection (targeted ethnic, regional, demographic audiences), see W. Bender, *Community and Personalization*, http://www.media.mit.edu/projects/isj/Section B/367/htm.

[73] *Hutchins Commission Report* at 12-16.

[74] Lee Bollinger, *Why There Should Be an Independent Decennial Commission on the Press*, 1993 U. Chi. Legal Forum 1, 4.

Today ownership concentration on a large scale, which the Hutchins Commission bemoaned, seems less of a problem than competition on a small scale. And there seems less cause for concern with the power of a few owners (the Hearsts, Pulitzers) than with the power of the market: the "consumers" in today's niche market; the advertisers who support news and programming directed to those small markets; and the financial markets that influence the behavior of today's media conglomerates. The watchword is conglomeration, not monopoly; large scale in small units; financial control but not necessarily control over content. It is an increasingly bottom-up, not top-down, communication environment.

The Hutchins Commission expressed deep concerns about concentration and monopoly power.

"[T]he outstanding fact about the communications industry today is that the number of its units has declined. In many places the small press has been completely extinguished. . . . News-gathering is concentrated in three great press associations, and features are supplied from a central source by syndicates. . . . Throughout the communications industry the little fellow exists on very narrow margins."[75]

* * *

"The main causes of the trend toward concentration in the communication industries have been the advantages inherent in operating on a large scale using the new [and mass market] technology."[76]

* * *

"The agencies of mass communication are big business, and their owners are big businessman. . . . As William Allen White put it, 'Too often the publisher of an American newspaper has made his

---

[75] *Hutchins Commission Report* at 37.

[76] *Hutchins Commission Report* at 48.

money in some other calling than journalism. He is a rich man seeking power and prestige.'"[77]

The same point was made with equal force by another distinguished editor, Virginius Dabney of the *Richmond Times-Dispatch*, writing in the *Saturday Review of Literature*:

"Today newspapers are Big Business, and they are run in that tradition. The publisher, who often knows little about the editorial side of the operation, usually is one of the leading business men in his community, and his editorial page, under normal circumstances, strongly reflects that point of view. . . . He looks upon the paper primarily as a 'property' rather than as an instrument for public service. . . . Of course, such a publisher sees that the editorials in his paper are 'sound', which is to say that they conform to his own weird views of society, and are largely unreadable."[78]

Many of these symptoms are familiar. But if the symptoms often appear the same today, the diagnosis is different. The *Hutchins Commission Report* was written at a time when the mass market dominated corporate behavior, and when, with monopoly power, the owner could control the mass market by creating single firms on a large scale and influence content through the power of ownership. With but few remaining exceptions, the mass market is a relic, at least in the news business. Today the prized market is not large, but small; not the mass market, but the niche market. And the strategy is not to achieve economies of large scale, but instead to focus on the new economies of small scale, economies achieved not through reaching everyone, but through reaching demographically and socioeconomical targeted markets for which the advertiser will pay a handsome premium.

We are today in the midst of a shift in the competitive paradigm in the communications industry. The structure of

---

[77] *Hutchins Commission Report* at 59.

[78] *Hutchins Commission Report* at 60-61.

competition in a market is premised on the economics of the market. In the first half of the 20th century the economic conditions in the communications market were those of the industrial revolution: high fixed costs most profitably spread over large volume, and a large, relatively homogenous market of news consumers. Large scale, in other words, was the paradigm to which competition drove firms, as if by a force of economic gravity.

Today the paradigm is reversing itself because the underlying economic forces are turning upside down. Fixed costs are low, variable costs are high. As a result, now the economies are the economies of small scale and specialization, not large scale and mass production. Competition in the communications industry, therefore, is being driven by economic gravitational pulls toward the specific and away from the general; toward the small unit and away from the large; toward labor- and technology-intensity and away from fixed-capital intensity; toward decentralization and away from centralization.

Signs of the shift can be seen everywhere. But they are most notable, though not most dramatic, in the newspaper industry, both the first and last bastion of the general audience served by news of general interest and importance. Many newspapers have been happily, if not eagerly, shedding circulation, becoming purposefully smaller rather than larger, yet more profitable.[79] This dramatic shift in mentality is due to market fragmentation, technology, intermedia competition, and advertiser influence, all of which are driven by the reversal of underlying economic forces in the communications industry. It is due, as well, to the newspaper's capacity economically to "unbundle," to disaggregate the separate markets and interests always attracted to the newspaper by comics, sports, features, local news, and so on.[80] In the past these special sections or features were used to "bundle" the paper–to draw a large and diverse audience to a

---

[79] See Chapter IV.

[80] For an interesting discussion of the economics of unbundling, see Katherine Fulton, *A Tour of Our Uncertain Future*, *supra* note 69.

single mass publication. But the "bundles" can also be disaggregated, serving as a useful means of breaking down an audience to serve advertiser interests and to generate greater subscription revenue.

Even more interesting, because counterintuitive to those trained in an industrial-revolution economic model, is the fact that the radical shift toward smaller circulation is intended simultaneously to increase revenue and decrease costs, thus delivering a double bonus to profitability. How is this happening?

First, with the shedding of circulation–and more specifically the shedding of (or unwillingness to seek) circulation in high-cost and low-income markets (such as rural areas or urban ghettos or minority communities)–the remaining, often upscale, customers can be, and are being, charged more for the newspaper. Pricing is not driven by a decreasing marginal-cost equation by which smaller increases in marginal revenue from new increments of circulation are justified because the marginal costs are very low. With low fixed costs today the equation is being reversed. Increased revenue per unit can more than offset the decline in units sold. And with upscale demographics there is a kicker. Most customers actually pay their bills, on time, too!

But the economics are more sophisticated than this simple marginal cost-and-revenue calculus. The second thing that happens is that advertisers, and especially those seeking upscale customers, are willing to pay premium rates for the efficient delivery of the new audience demographic, which is high income, high education, high taste.[81] And more of these most desirable advertisers will purchase advertising space in the more focused newspaper market. So while circulation goes down, and subscription revenues rise (or at least offset those lost at lower prices with the circulation decline), advertising revenue actually increases. And advertising revenues represent about 80 percent of the average newspaper's total revenue.[82]

Third, and finally, costs go down because a smaller number of newspapers need to be produced to serve the self-consciously

---

[81] See Chapter IV *supra*.

[82] See Chapter II *supra*.

reduced circulation. News staff, too, might be cut, because fewer people are needed to gather a more restricted body of information demanded by a narrower and more homogeneous audience.

This may sound all too cynical to be true, but it is actually happening, especially in the newspaper business. And this dramatic, indeed radical, shift of economic forces is influencing the structure of competition among newspapers and in the larger communication industry. It is doing so in ways that help explain the equally dramatic change that is occurring in the shape of concentration. With forces now tending toward small scale, decentralization, and specialization in market and audience, the former trend toward large scale, integration, centralization, and monopoly has now become a trend toward conglomeration of small and specialized units, spanning many markets and media rather than dominating one, searching out the niche rather than the mass market. It is toward audience- and market-based publications that are important not so much for their public value, but instead as instruments of revenue and advertising. The "news" that counts is the news that attracts and appeals to a small and defined audience. News, in other words, is simply the product, changeable at will, by which commerce is achieved. It is driven by, indeed defined by, that commerce: the need for revenues, the need for financial performance, the need to appeal to the widely-dispersed and institutionally dominated public ownership of the newspaper holding company, which is abstracted from the operating newspaper as if to reinforce the mere instrumentality of the commodity of news.

With this change in the economics of news has come a shift of power over content–power over information and news–from the owner and the editor to the advertiser and the audience. In a market controlled by monopoly owners, editorial judgment was possible, though often skewed by the preferences of the owners. Indeed, in a mass market editorial judgment was necessary, for the selection of news content for a large audience of diverse tastes was an economic imperative. The power of the monopolist was also, notably, the power to publish that which people, given a free choice, would *not* select.

Today's segmented market is more closely controlled by the audience, with the audience's preferences made more dominant by the demands of the advertisers.[83] That dominance is reinforced by a financial market sensitively tuned to the short-term demands of audience and advertiser.[84] In such a market, editorial judgment– choice of information the audience doesn't want, but needs–is much more constrained. As Robert Entman put it recently:[85]

"[I]n the real commercial market, the media do not create an information supply that resembles the metaphorical vision of a buzzing marketplace of ideas."

"Economists would call this an externality problem. Externalities are the unintended effects of market exchanges. For my purposes. . ., the most important externality . . . is the impact of the commercial market on civic interest and knowledge. The commercial market underproduces news that enhances citizens' political interest, knowledge, and sophistication, in large part because the commercial pressure on suppliers is to attract the largest audience possible. The average audience member does not seek complex, sophisticated information, and the mass media must target that average member. Without a more socially-useful idea supply in the mass media, consumers remain too uninformed to demand such a supply. The externality reinforces itself."

From an economic perspective, that is, editorial judgment and good news coverage are contrary to the market; if a newspaper

---

[83] The impact of audience attitudes on advertiser behavior, which in turn can influence the behavior of a publisher, particularly in a narrow market where the publisher is highly dependent on a select few advertisers, has been remarked upon frequently. See Bruce Owen and Steven Wildman, Video Economics (1992). A recent illustration was Chrysler's decision not to advertise on the television series "Ellen" because of its gay and lesbian content. See James B. Stewart, *Coming Out at Chrysler*, July 21, 1997, at 38.

[84] See Chapter IV *supra*.

[85] Robert Entman, *Putting the First Amendment in Its Place: Enhancing American Democracy Through the Press*, 1993 U. Chi. Legal Forum 61, 76.

supplies people with information they need in forms they can put to use, rather than information that they want in comfortable forms, there is no economic reason for the market to support it, as people won't, given choices, choose the better news over the worse. This is why, by traditional wisdom, news is separated from the advertising, sales, and other aspects of media firms, as profit motives must be muted, if not held at bay. News does not maximize profits, at least if it is news marked by sound and consistent editorial judgment about information people *need* to have.

In a mass market characterized by concentration, separation of news from sales was possible, for the large news organization had power independent of the market. But when the economies of scale are reversed, when the niche market replaces the mass market, and when competition intensifies, editorial judgment becomes more difficult to sustain. The audience's preferences must be more completely sated. And finally the breakdown of barriers between the news function and the economics of the enterprise occurs. Control over news cannot, in the new newspaper industry, be given over to journalism as historically practiced. It must be, and today is increasingly becoming, melded into the sales product that the newspaper, sadly, has come to be.

* * *

The engine of freedom of the press and journalism in the United States is editorial judgment: independent selection and composition of information judged by standards of public need, not private prejudice or personal gain. Editorial judgment is the substrata upon which news is built; it is the essential justification for an editor's or a writer's liberty to communicate current information and opinion to an audience. It accounts for much of the advantage that a free press has made possible; for the relative lack of corruption in government; for the consent of a people to our form of democratic government. The Hutchins Commission can be rightly criticized for failing to emphasize editorial judgment or to probe its meaning and its central role in accomplishing many of the aims set out by the commission.

Today editorial judgment is in jeopardy. The source of the jeopardy is the new combination of economic and technological forces bearing on the selection decisions now made in news organizations. These forces are making it increasingly difficult to rest news decisions on independent judgments oriented to public need rather than self-interest or raw consumer demand. The press' constitutional freedom was not fought in the name of target marketing and demographic market segmentation, and it was certainly not intended to foster news by market survey and focus group. It was fought in the name of intellectually honest, even occasionally brave, decisions about what is important and what the public needs, not wants, to know.

Chapter VI

Fettering Capitalism: Some Recommendations

A. Is Change Possible or Desirable?

A certain degree of helplessness and frustration confronts anyone concerned with the changes in the newspaper today, and particularly the changes in the newspapers owned by the publicly traded newspaper companies. Two persistent and, perhaps, unanswerable questions produce the sense of helplessness.

1. The Role of Economic Forces

The first question is whether the causes of the changes we have noted are truly the behaviors and incentives of the firm, or whether they are instead the ineluctable products of economic and technological forces. Perhaps the publicly traded companies are simply responding at a quickened pace to forces that in the end will affect all newspapers. There is much evidence to support this thesis. The technologies of gathering information, of compiling it, of composing it, and of distributing it to audiences have been transformed. The sources of information that newspapers transform into news on the pages are becoming centralized, produced in large and efficient enterprises and then made available to local newspapers in great variety.

The composition and distribution of newspapers are likewise changing radically. The economies of scale that once dictated a large and mass readership for a single newspaper product have been largely reversed. Computer and printing technology permit the printing of local editions adapted to the demands of small markets, markets dictated not so much by geography but instead by other criteria such as age and income and interest. In the rapidly changing technologies of distribution these editions may soon be capable of delivery on a finely-honed scale. This is already possible, of course, through computer technology, for those who want an "Internet" edition of the paper. Printing technology at the level of the individual home will soon make possible the delivery of a specifically adapted edition for each customer without the intervention of a news carrier, but instead by sending the paper to a printer in the subscriber's home, or through the use of news carriers equipped with technology that allows them easily to deliver a different edition at each door.

In these and other respects, then, technology is transforming the very identity of a "newspaper." Technology, of course, would not make such a transformation occur, but when combined with the economic benefits it can deliver, technology makes radical change all but inevitable.

In America advertising has been the lifeblood of the press almost from the very beginning. Over time, advertising revenues have accounted for an ever greater percentage of the newspaper's total revenue. During the course of the past 25 years, with newspaper readership consistently declining, advertising revenue has assumed an even greater role, accounting today for 75-80 percent of revenues in a typical newspaper. Readership consists more and more heavily of the better-educated and more affluent segments of communities, segments that also tend to consume the products of a capitalist society most heavily. With fewer but, for advertising purposes, better readers, and with advertisers willing to pay the highest rates (in relation to circulation) for ads that can be finely targeted to this heavily consuming sector, newspapers are understandably drawn to technologies that permit narrow and targeted audiences to be reached.

Technologies have thus complemented economic forces, driving newspapers to be more market oriented in their audiences and content, leading newspapers to segment and focus their markets, varying their products (editions, for example) to do so. These forces are so far less evident in the small town newspapers, which still publish to their small-scale mass markets, but the economies of scale in production and advertising are nevertheless at work, and many of these small papers are becoming part of large newspaper companies that specialize in maximizing their unique economies of scale.

What this brief synopsis suggests is that the basic forces of technology and economics, not the self-conscious and chosen behaviors of the newspaper chains, account for much of the change in the newspaper over the past 25 years, and especially over the past 10 to 15 years. Yet these technologies, inevitable as their forces may be, need not have driven newspapers in the particular direction they have taken. The technologies could also have been employed in ways that maximize the opportunities for news, that facilitate publication of even more complete and engaging and useful information upon which the newspaper readership has traditionally relied. And indeed, in some instances, this is precisely what has happened. Many people feel that the quality of news, especially national and regional news, has improved in the smaller-market papers owned by some of the chains. And there is no doubt that the variety of news sources available to anyone with a computer hooked up to the Internet has vastly improved. There are a number of newspaper chains, and a number of papers, that have employed technology to improve the news quality of their newspapers.

The publicly traded newspaper companies, however, have, with a few notable exceptions, taken a different course. Their course has been to employ technology and economic efficiencies single mindedly in pursuit of increased revenues, reduced costs, and always improving investment performance. These companies, in other words, adopted efficiencies and deployed technology with insufficient regard to the quality of their newspapers, and with excessive regard to investor demands and quarterly profits. This is a ruthless, and one might hope ultimately self-defeating, strategy, especially in an industry in which the barriers to entry by competitors are falling rapidly. But it is too often the strategy taken by firms whose focus has been transformed, perhaps in small and invisible increments, from news to business.

So while the underlying forces of technology and economics cannot reasonably be reversed, there are reasons to believe that changes can be made in the way in which these forces are employed in the large newspaper companies, and especially in the publicly traded companies. This, at least, is the premise underlying the suggestions for change and reform that we make in the pages that follow.

2. Are We Simply Getting What We Want?

The second question that must be confronted before recommending remedies to the problems in the newspaper business is whether the newspapers today are simply better reflections of what people want, whether or not some might consider the papers to be worse or of degraded quality. In a capitalist system, of course, the market is assumed to provide what people want, and when it does so, the end product is deemed both acceptable as a normative matter and likely preferable to what collective action, usually government, would provide. This same assumption has been understood by the Supreme Court to be the fundamental premise of the First Amendment. There are limitations to this principle, however, and one is of particular relevance to this study.

The First Amendment, the Supreme Court says, rests on a free market in ideas and information; a free press, moreover, is the "bulwark of liberty" essential, as David Anderson has put it, "'to the security of freedom in a state' ... provid[ing] a necessary restraint on what the patriots viewed as government's natural tendency toward tyranny and despotism."[86] The press's role is to provide needed information and opinion about public and private matters. These roles require the press to be free and independent of government, but they may require a measure of freedom from private markets, too, insofar as the private markets do not always place value, in the short run at least, on the oftentimes controversial, unsettling, and unwelcome gaze of the press's eye. The operation of the free market justifies a rule prohibiting government intervention in the news, its quality, or its content. But the free market must, in fact, operate if this rule is to make sense. The antitrust laws, the Supreme Court has said, can be applied to the press despite the First Amendment, because those laws are designed to protect the operation of the free market that represents the very premise of freedom of the press itself. Structural government regulation designed to protect the operation of

---

[86] David A. Anderson, *The Origins of the Free Press Clause*, 30 U.C.L.A. L.Rev. 455, 533 (1983).

the capitalist assumptions of the First Amendment, in other words, is acceptable, perhaps even necessary.

A problem of similar nature may exist in the publicly traded newspaper industry, leading to the conclusion that the competitive market in information and ideas is not working openly and freely in the newspaper industry, and therefore that the newspaper product we now see can't be explained simply as "what we want." The competitive market in ideas and information assumes that the providers of ideas and information are competing for, and responding to, the preferences of the consumers of ideas and information. If the newspapers don't provide what the readers want, they will change what they provide in order to retain the readers and, most important, the subscription revenues they provide.

But this model appears not to fit the publicly traded newspapers today, for two reasons. First, the market to which the newspapers are responding, from top to bottom of the organization, from business to news departments, is the stock market and the market demands of the passive investors who own the publicly traded stock in the companies. This is the point of our analysis of the incentives that have been set in place and that are shaping, in often unconscious ways, the goals and priorities and values of the firms. The stock market is not the market to which the First Amendment's metaphorical "marketplace of ideas and information" refers. The stock market measures the financial performance of a newspaper company, not the appeal or value of its news content. This may explain, in part, the apparent paradox of vastly increased profitability and financial-market performance in the face of circulation declines and increasing signs of public and reader dissatisfaction with the newspaper's content and concerns about the credibility with which newspapers perform their critical function in a free society.[87]

---

[87] See, for example, the report entitled *Examining Our Credibility: Why Newspaper Credibility Has Been Dropping*, published by the Journalism Credibility Project of the American Society of Newspaper Editors (1998); and the report entitled *Changing Definitions of News: A Look at the Mainstream Press Over 20 Years*, by the Project for Excellence in Journalism (1998).

Second, the newspapers owned by the publicly traded companies are dependent not on subscription revenues from the readers, but instead on the increasing and very dominant proportion of advertising revenue. The market's preference for the newspaper's content is thus being reflected not in the direct measure of consumer (reader) preference, but in the indirect (at best) measurement of advertiser satisfaction. To be sure, advertisers are responsive to the consumers, for it is the consumers whom the advertisers want to reach. But there are two, largely systemic, problems with using this fact to support the conclusion that the consumers' preferences are being reflected. Advertisers are interested in the consumers' buying practices, not their reading preferences. In a market where there aren't a lot of competing newspapers, buying preferences are a pretty obscure and imperfect approximation of consumer preferences for news content and quality. More basically, advertisers are interested only in the preferences of some consumers, those who buy their products. They are indifferent to the preferences of readers who are not consumers. Thus to the extent that advertisers will serve as a surrogate for consumer preferences, visiting their measure of those preferences on the newspapers with which they do business, the preferences thus manifested will not be those of a general reading public, but of specific segments of it. Newspapers may respond to these advertiser preferences by shedding audience and adapting the news product to the narrow preferences of those targeting subsets of the community. And this, it appears, is indeed precisely what newspapers, and especially the publicly traded newspapers, have done.

So newspapers are not simply a reflection of what we want, a reflection of our preferences judged by a neutral and efficient capitalist market. Instead, an important qualification must be stated. Newspapers are increasingly a reflection of what *the advertisers tell the newspapers that some of us* want, which is what the financial markets tell the newspapers they want. The rest of us have less to say about the matter. In a world of increasing choices among the sources of information we want–television, radio, magazines, bulletin boards, talk rooms, newspapers, and thousands of sites on the Internet–it can be argued that this qualification is not a matter for concern.

Newspapers are simply becoming a specialized and focused medium like magazines or film, to name but two traditionally narrow sources of information.

But it must also be said that newspapers have historically served as the main, perhaps the only, broadly democratic and broadly representative source of information in our democratic society. Indeed, the trends in newspaper news away from hard news and toward "featurized and people-oriented approach[es] . . . [and] lifestyle, celebrity, entertainment and celebrity crime/scandal"[88] reflect not a shift in hard news to alternative media, but instead a movement by newspapers toward the shallower and more visceral news now dominant in the other media. The transformation of newspapers is therefore clearly a cause for concern, especially if no comparable (in breadth and quality and durability) medium of information is taking the newspaper's place.

B. Recommendations for Change

Given the foregoing, it might be expected that we would urge publicly traded newspaper companies to revert to private ownership. We do not, because (1) private ownership does not necessarily assure a commitment to quality journalism; (2) the problems we identify can, we think, be addressed through organizational and structural changes within the public firm; and (3) the recommendations that follow are less drastic and more likely ways to encourage a press committed to public service.[89] Two premises underlie our recommendations. The first is that the changes we have identified are not simply the end products of technological and economic determinism. They are not, in short, inevitable. We take technological and economic change as a given, but conclude that the

---

[88] Project for Excellence in Journalism, *Changing Definitions of News: A Look at the Mainstream Press Over 20 Years*, at 2 (1998).

[89] "Going private" also may put a company "in play," resulting in unwanted takeover bids.

direction of that change is only partly a product of those forces; it is also partly a product of other structural, but less fundamental, forces, such as investment markets, incentives built into the firm, and short-run orientation that tends to discount the value of quality and to frustrate the newspaper's continued ability to perform its most important public functions.

The second premise is that the new newspaper product–shorter on broad news coverage, softer in content, adapted to a narrower audience, oriented to advertising efficiency–is not so much a reflection of what we want, not really a reflection of a market of consumers, but is instead a reflection of what advertisers desire in a market of passive and return-maximizing investors who are otherwise largely indifferent to the content of the news product. With these premises in mind, we offer a series of suggestions that may, in some combination, alter the direction of change, though not the fact of it.

1. Newspaper companies should adopt a number of changes in their business organization and operating practices.

>**a. Boards of directors should have more than one member who is a retired or active journalist of high repute and who does not work for the company.** At least one of these journalist board members should be on the compensation committee or the committee responsible for setting compensation policy in the firm, including compensation of executive management and compensation guidelines for editorial staff of the newspapers owned by the firm. Boards should also consider appointing a member who would serve, independently of management, as an ombudsman who maintains close familiarity with each of the company's newspapers and reports to the board on standards of quality for the newspapers and their accomplishment. This person should also serve on the compensation committee.

b. The board of directors should consist primarily of outsider members, persons not in executive positions with the firm or related to major institutional investors in the firm.

c. Except for directors who are employees of the company, directors should not receive compensation in the form of stock options or other incentives tied to stock market performance.

d. Bonus and other incentive compensation for executive management of the parent company responsible for the newspapers (including the chief executive officer and the chief operating officer of the company) should be based in significant part on the circulation and journalistic quality of the newspapers.

e. At least half of the incentive compensation for publishers of the company's newspapers should be based on criteria strictly related to circulation and journalistic quality.

f. Editorial management and news personnel of the newspapers should not receive any incentive compensation based on financial performance. If incentive compensation is extended to editorial and news personnel, it should be based strictly on circulation and journalistic quality. Incentive compensation, moreover, should consist only of bonuses and not include stock options, for stock options present a serious risk of conflict of interest for persons involved in the journalistic functions of the newspaper.

g. The company's standards of journalistic quality should be established in advance after consultation

with an external group of journalists and others who are knowledgeable about journalism. The specific judgments periodically made about news quality for purpose of incentive compensation should be based on regularized consultation with knowledgeable persons unaffiliated with the company, familiar with the community and the newspaper, and experienced in newspaper journalism. The standards of news quality should be available to the public and periodically published in the company's newspapers.

h. Each newspaper should maintain and report annually to the public both historic and current information on the following:

i. Total revenues, broken down by category (advertising, subscription, etc.).
ii. Total expenses, broken down into categories (news, production, advertising, distribution, etc.).
iii. Operating margin (total and percentage).
iv. Circulation, both total and broken down by areas or groups that the company tracks.
v. The names, titles, and qualifications of the members of the boards of directors of the parent company (this is currently public information but is not generally disseminated by the newspapers owned by the company).
vi. The names of persons or companies or funds that own more than two percent of the parent company's publicly traded stock.
vii. The compensation paid to the five highest paid employees of the parent company, and the compensation paid to the publisher and the three highest paid employees of the newspaper, including bonus and incentive compensation.

viii. The net profit and return on equity of the parent company (as reported to the SEC).

This information is already compiled on an ongoing basis by newspapers for reporting within the company and to industry reporting services (though it is not usually available to the public). It is, in other words, easily available and much of it is already distributed within the industry. Given the public interest in the performance of the press, there is little justification, practical or legal, for withholding it from the public which, in a free market, should be enabled to make educated choices about the news it receives and selects.

2. The holding period for capital-gains treatment for common stocks in publicly traded newspaper companies should be extended to at least one, and preferably to two or even more, years.[90]

---

[90] Our recommendation that the holding period for capital-gains treatment be extended for newspaper-company stocks reflects the scope of our study and is not intended to imply that the holding period should not be extended for other company stocks. Indeed, an increased tax incentive for gains on stock held more than five years has recently been enacted by Congress. We have not studied the arguments that might apply to other companies, and leave it to those who have done so to advance that case. In any event, we believe that an extension of the holding period for newspaper company stocks alone could be justified constitutionally because of the special informing role played by newspapers. *See* Leathers v. Medlock, 499 U.S. 439 (1991) (sustaining constitutionality of exception to general sales tax for newspapers, but not cable broadcasters); Randall Bezanson, Taxes on Knowledge in America: Exactions on the Press from Colonial Times to the Present, 267-85 (U. Penn. Press 1994).

This change would be conducive to attracting investors with longer-term horizons that are not affected by quarterly results and short-term market performance, thus making the stocks less volatile. The stocks would thus be less useful for short-term incentive compensation. Investors may be more interested in the long-term strength and value of the company, which, we believe, rests heavily on the quality of the news published by its newspapers. Consideration should be given to extending the tax benefits of the extended holding period to institutional investors (such as pension funds) that do not presently receive benefits because of their tax status.

3. Legal changes should be effected to assure that directors of the companies are authorized to consider the journalistic quality of the newspapers and the needs of the communities served by them in making business decisions, including decisions about acquisition and sale of the company and any of its newspapers.

Legal standards now applied in many states may permit the boards to consider such matters, though the matter is in some flux and greater certainty would be desirable.[91]

4. Government policy toward newspaper competition should be changed from one that protects newspapers against competition to one that permits and even fosters competition.

---

[91] See, for example, the potentially conflicting decisions of the Delaware Supreme Court in Revlon, Inc. v. MacAndrews & Forbes Holdings, Inc., 506 A.2d 173, 176 (1985) (consideration of constituencies and interests other than shareholder value can be taken only as long as "there [is] some rationally related benefit accruing to the stockholders"), and in Paramount Communications, Inc. v. Time Incorporated, 571 A.2d 1140, 1145-46, 1150 (1989) (Time, Inc.'s board could elect a merger with lower value to the shareholders because, inter alia, it afforded the opportunity to preserve the autonomy and quality of its journalistic operations).

Much government policy toward newspapers has been geared toward preserving them, by isolating them and their markets and protecting them in ways that eliminate competition. Government policy has been protectionist, designed to prevent rather than to foster or permit competition.[92]

Examples of this policy are the Joint Operating Agreements that have been expressly permitted as a matter of federal law. These agreements permit competing newspapers in a market to combine non-news operations in order to protect them against failure.[93]

In a similar vein, antitrust policy has been extremely lax, if not non-existent, in the newspaper merger and acquisition field. This is a reflection of the very same policy that underlies the authorization of joint operating arrangements, a policy premised on the assumption that in the long and short run communities simply cannot sustain more than one newspaper and, as a consequence, government policy should protect against, rather than foster, the continuation or emergence of competition.

In many ways the government policy of protectionism toward newspapers has failed. It has failed to encourage competition *based on the news product*, though it has permitted other forms of competition–weeklies, alternative newspapers, magazines, books, and of course broadcast and Internet technologies. The government policy, then, has become largely irrelevant in the new competitive climate.

Yet even in this new environment, daily newspapers retain a significant mass market–perhaps more significant than any other medium for news–largely because, one suspects, they are relatively cheap, printed and easy to read, and they cover a broad range of information that no other medium publishes on an ongoing basis.

---

[92] See, e.g., the "Newspaper Preservation Act," 15 U.S.C. §1801 et. seq. (1970); *Joint Operating Agreements in the Newspaper Industry: A Threat to First Amendment Freedoms*, 138 U. Pa. L. Rev. 275 (1989); Mich. Cit. for an Indep. Press v. Thornburgh, 868 F.2d 1285, 1297 (D.C. Cir. 1989) (Ginzburg, dissenting).

[93] Id.

There may be no reason, in short, to declare the death of printed daily news. It remains viable and, more important, profitable. While its form and the ways in which it will be distributed will surely change, the "newspaper" continues to attract a large and persistent readership who depend on it for a broad range of professionally selected information on political, social, and economic matters.

If this means, as many believe, that the newspaper will continue to thrive, a policy geared toward preventing competition–especially competition in terms of the breadth and quality of information provided–is short-sighted. It reinforces monopoly power, enabling newspapers to be less attentive to their audiences and the quality of their product. It thus ultimately disserves the interests of readers, the public, and the goals of a free press.

We therefore recommend a reversal of government regulatory policy toward newspaper competition, changing it from one of protecting newspapers from competition to a policy that encourages competition and restrains monopoly power.

5. Encourage the development of alternative forms of newspaper companies at the community level that will be more long-run oriented, less profit-driven, more responsive to readership needs; in short, companies that will practice better journalism.

Such organizational arrangements could serve, for the owners, as an alternative to the sale of local newspapers to the public chains; they could also serve as a corporate form for current or new competing news companies (whatever form their news product might take). If such newspaper firms are created, they could be more expressly devoted to news and news quality; they could also, even if only by example, serve as a form of competition for the public and chain-owned papers, with the terms of competition being the completeness and quality of news. Given a choice, we believe people will select the newspaper that provides the best news content.

A variety of forms are possible, ranging from the locally owned for-profit newspaper company, to the non-profit newspaper company, to the charitable corporation dedicated to educational purposes, to the cooperative corporation. None of these are new forms of organization. Most exist in some form in the news business. The locally owned for-profit newspaper, of course, exists in many communities throughout the country today, though the number of such locally owned independent papers is dwindling rapidly as the public companies and chains are eager to purchase them for very high prices, thus luring the owners to sell, or all but forcing their sale to pay estate taxes when a principal owner dies. A few newspapers are nonprofit companies. An example is Independent Newspapers, Inc., a non-profit holding company devoted to owning independent newspapers devoted to high standards of journalism and operated in a spirit of public trust, which in turn owns a number of community newspapers that operate as for-profit companies but whose profits are reinvested in the newspapers in order to support the company's mission. Not-for-profit companies are free from income taxes so long as they do not accumulate excessive retained earnings, and are freer than for-profit firms to devote their attention to community needs and news quality, objectives defined in their corporate charters.

Many news organizations are charitable organizations, exempt from federal and state taxes and able to give their contributors income tax deductions for individual contributions. Perhaps the most common news organizations taking this form are public television and radio stations, many of which are free-standing corporations, many others of which are parts of a larger educational institution, such as a university. High school and university newspapers devoted to education are often (though less frequently with universities) tax exempt charitable organizations. And a number of formerly profit-making newspapers have been changed into charitable corporations, often at the death of the founder/owner who wished to preserve the paper and devote its income to charitable institutions. The *St. Petersburg Times* is perhaps the most well known example,[94] but

---

[94] Paul C. Tash, *St. Petersburg Times* editor and president, describes his company's journalism and business outlook this way:

> "Profits are the means, not the end. We need to make a buck to keep the business strong, because that business supports good journalism. But we're not in

there are other examples, such as the *New London Day*.⁹⁵ Finally, a large number of specialized news publications are owned and

> business simply to make a buck. Our commitment to a first-rate news report is itself a business strategy. *The Times* is now the largest daily newspaper in Florida. Only a third of the *St. Petersburg Times'* circulation [340,000 daily, 440,000 Sunday] is in St. Petersburg, and that happened because we became home-town papers for lots of places beyond our home town. We committed substantial resources to covering those communities. We devote at least 40 percent of our news budget to local news, much of which goes to only a portion of our audience. To help attract a capable staff, we find ourselves paying full-run rates for part-run news.
>
> "Our overall news budget could be described as generous–except that we regard it as a central element of the business strategy. We have roughly 400 full-time news staff. News spending represents about one-seventh of total expenses for the company, and exceeds one-tenth of total revenue–rough measures of news as a proportion of the enterprise.
>
> "If we were trying to maximize quarterly profits, to please Wall Street analysts or a distant owner, such long-term investment strategy would be impossible. We never could have expanded the newspaper into what turned out to be very important markets, because such growth would have diluted profits in the short- to medium-term."

⁹⁵ The *Day*, daily circulation 42,000, surpasses other papers in its circulation category by virtually every objective measure of newspaper quality: news-editorial expense as a percent of total newspaper revenue; number of news-editorial employees; average salary per full-time equivalent; number of pages of news-editorial content and percentage of space devoted to newshole.

published by charitable or educational or cultural institutions, serving their membership and clientele and communities.

The cooperative corporation is most widely known for its presence in the public utilities industries, particularly in the upper Midwest. But cooperatives are not limited to electrical or gas or telephone companies. Many grocery stores are cooperatives. And in a loose sense many newsletters published by organizations such as labor unions are cooperative in nature, serving the membership and owned and controlled by the membership. With a cooperative the customers are the owners; prices are set at a level that generates modest income only, and that income is devoted either to the capital needs of the cooperative or returned to the customers or members. For a newspaper, a cooperative organization would work in much the same way. Like the Associated Press, subscribers would be the owners, whose interests would be pro-rated according to the amount of subscription payments they have made. The difficulty posed by a cooperative in a competitive environment is initial access to capital, for the initial investment can be high and, without an established customer base and base of advertising revenue, access to commercial loans is difficult. This is why, outside of the regulated-monopoly setting, cooperatives are not very common. When they do exist they will often have been initially funded by loans from individuals dedicated to the venture's success, and operating costs are held to a minimum by the use of volunteer labor by members of the cooperative. While start-up capital and high operating costs in the early stages of a cooperative would be a problem for a newspaper cooperative, neither seems more insurmountable for a newspaper than it would be in other industries where cooperatives have been successful. Moreover, the lower capital investment and start-up costs for most Internet, or online, business may make the emergence of local cooperative news organizations more likely in the future.

Regardless of the specific form a newspaper company might take, there are a number of specific steps that would encourage the development or survival of independent newspapers devoted to news quality as well as profit:

a. Assure that favorable tax treatment is available to non-profit news organizations, and that tax-exempt status is available for newspapers devoted to educational purposes. Such newspapers should be free from the current Internal Revenue Service constraint against editorializing on political campaign issues and candidates.[96]

b. Extend favorable estate- and income-tax treatment to the owners of newspapers who transfer the companies to a tax exempt educational institution or foundation. Favorable tax treatment should include the deductibility as a charitable contribution of the amount the shares would have been worth were the newspaper to have been sold on the market, as well as the option of conversion of common shares into a form or preferred debt security in the charitable corporation.

6. Re-examine recent changes in the securities laws and regulations that have permitted institutional investors–including particularly mutual funds and retirement funds that have large stakes in the companies and have great market leverage on stock performance–to have greater direct communication with the publicly traded newspaper companies, ongoing access to corporate information not generally available to the public, and influence on matters of corporate strategy and policy.

Whether or not these securities policies have had an effect on the operation of the public companies in the past, there is no reason

---

[96] Notwithstanding the current IRS rules against endorsing candidates and taking positions on candidates and campaign issues, the Supreme Court has already held, in *FCC v. League of Women Voters*, 468 U.S. 364 (1968), that in the more closely regulated broadcast medium such restrictions against editorializing violate the First Amendment.

for these large investors to have effectively advantageous access and influence, and there is a risk that such ongoing involvement with the newspaper companies will exacerbate the companies' dominant financial market orientation and short-term outlook.

C. Conclusion

The function performed by newspapers throughout their history, a history that also corresponds with the history of the press and its freedom, is the broadly democratic one of providing a common record of information and opinion upon which people depend for the conduct of their political, social, cultural, and economic affairs. Today newspapers remain the primary medium through which these functions are realized, for they provide broad and deep coverage of events and people and government, to all people, and in a form that can be preserved. Newspapers, by definition, exclude none from access to their pages.

It would be a mistake to assume, and certainly to predicate recommendations upon, the perpetual existence of newspapers as we know them. Forces of economics and technology are changing and will continue to change the form, the content, and the manner of distribution of current news. In a real sense the publicly traded newspaper companies are both instruments and engines of these changes, and there is no reason to believe that the resting point of change in the form news takes will be less than benign by virtue of their serving as its instrument. Large firms have usually dominated the newspaper business, often leading the way for change. Form, in short, is likely to take care of itself and to be driven by forces that can't, in the end, be resisted.

But the public function of the newspaper, the publishing of a broad range of information and opinion to all, cheaply, on matters deemed important in the professional judgment of editors–must be preserved. Our concern in this study is with function, not form. In the publicly traded newspaper organizations, at least, a new market, the stock market, is pulling the strings. With something akin to a gravitational force, new incentives have been introduced throughout the firms, and in the news operations of the firms: incentives geared to segmenting markets along class and interest and income lines, thus compromising the goal of producing news useful to and available to all; incentives geared to maximizing margins and profits even at the expense of news; incentives reinvigorated at quarterly intervals when the financial markets pay attention and the investors most care; incentives geared to revenue and, thus, inevitably to advertiser interest and advertising efficiency, not to reader or community interest or need.

News has always been a business. There are sufficient reasons (private control, independence from government) to hope that it will always be so. But the business of the news business has, first and foremost, been news–its usefulness, its quality, its vitality, its attractiveness to readers. News and business have coexisted. As a general matter, both have prospered.

Our concern is that today, in the publicly traded newspaper company, the business of news is being transformed into the business of business. News is not its product, upon which the enterprise depends for its long-term survival. News is instead increasingly an instrument by which advertisers are lured, customers are efficiently reached, advertising rates are increased, news staff is cut, and margins are increased, and increased, and increased. At its worst, the publicly traded newspaper company, its energy entirely drawn to the financial market's unrealistic and greedy expectations, can become indifferent to news and, thus, ultimately to the fundamental purposes served by news and the press.

Some of the publicly traded companies are today acting as if news were dispensable if only a more efficient means of reaching customers could be found; they are acting as if they see themselves as simply a channel for consumption, a broker and distributor of commerce. Others continue, in some or even large measure, to retain a commitment to news as their business, and to remain successful and profitable as well. If there are ways to encourage companies to follow the latter example, not the former, shouldn't they be taken? Our continued capacity to realize fully the purposes served by a free press may be at stake.

Appendix A

Company Information

A.H. Belo Corporation

The A.H. Belo Company dates to 1842. As of 1999, it owned six daily newspapers with a combined circulation of 910,000. It also owned 17 television stations, reaching 14.3 percent of the U.S. television households, managed four television stations, and owned four local or regional cable news channels. Its newspaper segment accounted for 56 percent of the company's revenues; broadcasting accounted for 43.3 percent.

The A.H. Belo Corporation went public in 1981. It has two classes of stock. Series A shareholders have one vote per share; Series B shareholders have 10 votes per share. Three family members own more than 50 percent of Series B shares, which in turn control 85 percent of the total voting power.

The A.H. Belo board of directors is large, with 14 members, down two from 1998. Three family members serve on the board. Four members of the board have experience working in media companies; one has significant journalism experience.

Non-employee directors receive an annual compensation package of $85,000 ($90,000 for committee chairs). One-half of this amount is paid in stock options for Series B shares. Directors may elect to receive all or a portion of the remaining amount in additional stock options.

Newspaper publishing revenues increased 13 percent in 1998 to $788 million. Advertising revenues accounted for 85 percent of total newspaper revenues in 1998; circulation revenues accounted for 12 percent, and commercial printing contributed the remainder. The company's net revenues increased 12.7 percent between 1997 and 1998. Net income dropped 21.8 percent over the same time period, from $83 million to $64.9 million.

Between 1988 and 1997, the company's net revenues increased by 265.2 percent. Net income increased 543.1 percent. Net revenue for its newspaper and broadcasting segments increased at similar levels. Broadcasting revenues increased 268.4 percent between 1988 and 1998; newspaper revenues increased 257.9 percent over the same time period. In 1988, newspapers accounted for 57.1 percent of the company's revenues and broadcasting 42.9 percent. In 1998, newspapers accounted for 56 percent of total revenues and broadcasting 43.3 percent. Between 1988 and 1998, operating profit margins rose from 11.1 percent to 16.6 percent. But profit margins fluctuated considerably over this time period, ranging from a low of 11.1 percent to a high of 20.9 percent.

Between 1992 and 1997, cumulative shareholder investment return was 183 percent, exceeding both the S&P 500 (151 percent) and the company's peer group (161 percent), which is composed of comparable newspaper companies. The price of a share of the company's stock increased by 486.9 percent between 1988 and 1997. The price-earnings ratio was 31 in 1997.

In 1999, 304 institutional investors owned 69.19 percent of the company's common stock. In 1998, 305 institutional investors owned 73.93 percent of the stock.

Mutual funds comprised 45.1 percent of the institutional investors, money managers 45.1 percent, banks 9.2 percent, insurance companies 3.6 percent, and colleges .3 percent. BankBoston Corp., the largest institutional investor, owned 6.82 percent of the stock. The 10 largest institutional investors owned 30.93 percent of the company's stock; the five largest, 21.12 percent. The two largest institutional investors owned 12.37 percent of the company's stock.

A.H. Belo

Ten Largest Institutional Investors, 1999

Institution	Type	Shares Owned	% of Total Shares
BankBoston Corp	MM	6,762,211	6.82%
Phoenix Investment Mgt	MM	5,504,828	5.55
Goldman Sachs & Company	MM	3,201,073	3.23
Equitable Cos.	IN	2,968,800	3.01
Luther King Cap	MM	2,481,509	2.50
Bristol, John W.	MM	2,343,860	2.36
Oak Valley Capital Mgt	MM	2,198,569	2.22
N & B	MM	2,047,676	2.07
Capital Res & Mgt	MM	1,600,000	1.61
Barclays Bank	BA	1,527,217	1.54

Central Newspapers

The Central Newspapers Company was formed in 1934 by Eugene Pulliam. In 1999 the company owned seven daily newspapers with a total circulation of 832,000. The company also owned an 80 percent share of the Westech group of companies, which organizes job fairs, publishes career magazines, and maintains a resume web site for the high-tech industry; an 80 percent share in Home Buyer's Fair LLC, which provides Internet based services and information for people who are moving and for corporations that are relocating employees; a direct-marketing services company and a minority interest in a newsprint mill and a commercial printer.

Central Newspapers went public in 1989. It has two classes of stock. Class A shareholders are entitled to one-tenth of a vote per share; class B shareholders to one vote per share. The Pulliam family, of which former Vice President Dan Quayle is a member, controls about 90 percent of the voting power through ownership of the company's Class B stock.

The company's principal line of business is newspaper publishing. Operating revenues from other sources accounted for 5.3 percent of the total revenues in 1998. In 1998, the company had record revenues, operating income, net income, earnings per share and earnings before taxes, depreciation and amortization (EBITDA).

Advertising revenues increased 3.9 percent between 1997 and 1998 and accounted for 74.7 percent of the company's revenues in 1998. Circulation revenues were up 5.1 percent between 1997 and 1998 and accounted for 20 percent of the company's revenues. Total revenues increased 5.1 percent over 1997.

Between 1988 and 1997, advertising revenues increased 66.5 percent; circulation revenues by 91.5 percent. Total revenues were up 72.5 percent for the 11-year period. Net income was up 205.4 percent and profit margins showed steady increases, from 10.9% in 1988 to 20.5 percent in 1998. Return on shareholder's equity dropped in the early 1990s, but recovered and steadily increased, surpassing 34 percent in 1998.

Three members of the seven-person Central Newspapers board have experience working for newspapers; two, both officers in the company, have significant journalism experience.

Non-employee members of the board receive an annual retainer of $20,000, plus $1,000 for each board meeting attended and $750 for each committee meeting attended. Each non-employee member receives an annual grant of stock options to purchase 1,000 shares of the company's class A common stock.

Between 1992 and 1997, the total cumulative return on investment for Central Newspapers was greater than the S&P 500 and the company's peer group, which is composed of comparable newspaper companies. Cumulative shareholder return for Central Newspapers was 243 percent, compared with 158 percent for the S&P 500 and 141 percent for the company's peer group. The price of a share of the company's stock increased 223.2 percent between 1988 and 1997. The price-earnings ratio was 20 in 1997.

From 1998 and 1999, the percentage of stock owned by institutional investors increased from 52.72 percent to 66.52 percent. The number of institutions, however, dropped from 200 in 1998 to 194 in 1999.

In 1999, mutual funds represented 52.1 percent of the institutional investors, money managers 39.2 percent, banks 7.2 percent, and insurance companies 1.6 percent. Ariel Capital Management, the largest institutional investor, owned 9.16 percent of the stock. The 10 largest institutional investors own 33.45 percent of the stock; the five largest, 23.13 percent.

Central Newspapers

Ten Largest Institutional Investors, 1999

Institution	Type	Shares Owned	% of Total Shares
Ariel Capital Management	MM	3,426,184	9.16%
Goldman Sachs & Company	MM	1,345,755	3.60
Harris Association	MM	1,322,326	3.50
Gardner Inv	MM	1,299,778	3.47
Babson (DL) & Co.	MM	1,271,840	3.40
Wellington Management	MM	985,300	2.63
Mutual Shares	MF	850,600	2.27
Barclays Bank	BA	742,656	1.98
Pioneer Fund	MF	640,600	1.71
Reich & Tang Asst	MM	629,950	1.68

Dow Jones & Company

The Dow Jones Company was founded in 1882. It owns (as of 1999) the *Wall Street Journal*, the *Asian Wall Street Journal*, the *Wall Street Journal Europe* and the *Wall Street Journal Americas*, which have a total circulation of 4.1 million. The company also owns *Barron's*. It owns 19 dailies with a total circulation of 568,000, and 15 weekly newspapers. The company owns Dow Jones Interactive Publishing, the Wall Street Journal Interactive Edition, and two radio services that produce business and financial reports for radio stations. The company also has a minority interest in a number of publishing and information companies in the United States and abroad.

The Dow Jones Company went public in 1963 and has two classes of stock. Common stock owners are entitled to one vote per share; Class B common shareholders are entitled to 10 votes per share. Members of the Bancroft family hold a controlling interest in the company through their control of Class B shares.

There are 15 persons on the Dow Jones & Company board of directors.

Board members receive $1,200 for each meeting of the board they attend; $1,000 for each committee meeting attended and an annual fee of $3,000 for chairing a committee. Each non-company director is credited with $20,000 worth of stock equivalents per year and is paid $20,000 in cash. The directors, however, may choose to defer receipt of any or all of the cash portion and either have it placed in an interest-bearing account or invested in shares of common stock.

Dow Jones realigned its business operations in 1998 into three segments: print publishing, electronic publishing and community newspapers. Print publishing includes the company's print publications (*The Wall Street Journal* and its international editions, *Barron's* and other periodicals) and television operations. It accounted for 62 percent of the company's revenues in 1998. Electronic publishing includes Dow Jones Newswires, Dow Jones Interactive Publishing and Dow Jones Indexes group. Electronic publishing accounted for 21 percent of the company's revenues in 1998. The community newspaper segment consists of its Ottaway Newspapers, Inc., subsidiary, which published 19 daily and 15 weekly newspapers as of 1998. The community newspaper segment accounted for 17 percent of the company's 1998 revenues.

Advertising revenues increased 1.9 percent from 1997 to 1998 and accounted for 47.8 percent of the company's total revenues. Circulation revenues were down .6 percent from 1997 to 1998 and accounted for 21.2 percent of the company's revenues. The company's revenues decreased 16.1 percent from 1997 to 1998.

Between 1988 and 1998, advertising revenues increased 50.3 percent; circulation revenues also increased 50.3 percent. Revenues increased 25.5 percent between 1990 and 1998. Net income and profit margins fluctuated between 1988 and 1998, with the highs for both occurring in 1988 and 1989. Operating profit margins dropped from a high of 22 percent in 1988 to 10.1 percent in 1998. (The company showed a loss in 1997 because of restructuring charges and a charge for impairment of value of Dow Jones market.)

Between 1992 and 1997, cumulative investment return for Dow Jones stock was below the S&P 500 and the S&P Publishing Index. Cumulative shareholder return was 125 percent, compared with 152 percent for the S&P 500 and 136 percent for the S&P Publishing Index. The price of a share of the company's stock increased by 82 percent between 1988 and 1997. The price-earnings ratio was 32 in 1997.

Institutional ownership of the company's stock dropped from 81.94 percent in 1998 to 74.49 percent in 1999. The number of institutional investors remained nearly the same, 418 in 1999 and 420 in 1998.

Mutual funds represented 55.3 percent of the institutional investors, money managers 32.1 percent, banks 9.3 percent, insurance companies 3.1 percent, and colleges .4 percent. Roy Hammer, the largest institutional investor, owned 9.56 percent of the stock. The 10 largest institutional investors owned 41.22 percent of the company's stock; the five largest, 29.61 percent.

Dow Jones & Company

Ten Largest Institutional Investors, 1999

Institution	Type	Shares Owned	% of Total Shares
Hammer Roy	MM	6,748,068	9.56%
State Street Corp	MM	5,459,547	7.74
Washington Mutual Investors	MF	3,267,500	4.63
Barclays Bank	BA	2,919,625	4.14
Lord Abbett Affiliated Fund Inc.	MF	2,500,000	3.54
Fundamental Investors Inc.	MF	2,317,800	3.28
Inv Co America	MF	2,000,000	2.83
T. Rowe Price Equitable Income	MF	1,300,000	1.84
Mutual Shares	MF	1,295,800	1.84
Dodge & Cox	MM	1,282,061	1.82

E.W. Scripps Company

E.W. Scripps Company is one of the oldest newspaper companies in the United States. As of 1999, it owned 19 daily newspapers with a total circulation of 1.3 million. The company also owned nine network-affiliated television stations, Home & Garden Television, the Television Food Network, and a 12 percent interest in FOX SportSouth, a regional cable television network. The company also syndicated and licensed news features and comics. The newspaper segment represented 59.5 percent of the company's revenues.

The company went public in 1998. Owners of Class A common stock elect one-third of the members of the board of directors and vote only on those matters that Ohio law requires. Holders of the Common Voting Shares elect two-thirds of the board of directors and vote on all company matters. There is no active market for the Common Voting Shares. The Edward W. Scripps Trust owns approximately 84 percent of these shares and 53 percent of Class A common stock. The trust will terminate upon the death of the last of four identified individuals (the youngest now being 74). Upon termination, the trust's assets will be distributed to a group of 28 grandchildren, some of whom have entered into an agreement to maintain control of the company.

The 10-person board of directors of E.W. Scripps Company is dominated by family members. Four members of the family sit on the board. Three of these family members have experience in journalism. The Edward W. Scripps Trust is also represented on the board.

Each non-employee member of the board receives an annual fee of $30,000 and an additional $2,000 for each meeting attended. Additionally, each director who is a committee chair receives an annual fee of $3,000. Beginning in 1999, non-employee directors will also receive annual nonqualified stock option awards of 2,000 shares.

E.W. Scripps is a diversified media company. Its newspaper operations accounted for 59.5 percent of its 1998 revenues. Advertising revenues accounted for 44.5 percent of total revenues in 1998 and were up 22.2 percent over 1997. Circulation revenues increased 18.1 percent from 1997 to 1998 and accounted for 10.5 percent of total revenues. Revenues were up 17.2 percent from 1997 to 1998.

Advertising and circulation revenues were flat or declined between 1988 and 1997, but increased significantly in 1998. Advertising revenues increased 26.1 percent and circulation revenues increased 10.1 percent between 1988 and 1998. Operating profit increased 46 percent and net income increased 87.3 percent over the 11-year period. Operating profit margins declined in the late 1980s, reaching a low of 12.1 percent in 1990s. Through the rest of the

1990s, profit margins steady improved, reaching a high of 20.2 percent in 1997.

The cumulative shareholder investment return for E.W. Scripps between 1992 and 1997 was greater than the return for the S&P 500 or the company's peer group, which is composed of comparable newspaper companies. Cumulative shareholders' return for Scripps was 238 percent, compared to 152 percent for the S&P 500 and 157 percent for the company's peer group. The price of the company's stock increased 23.0 percent between 1995 and 1997. The price-earnings ratio was 28 in 1997.

There were 194 institutional investors in owning 48.63 percent of the company's common stock in 1999. This compares to 182 institutional investors owing 48.81 percent of the stock in 1998.

In 1999, mutual funds represented 49.5 percent of all institutional investors, money managers 36.1 percent, banks 10.8 percent, insurance companies 3.1 percent, and colleges .5 percent. The largest institutional investor, Wellington Management, owned 3.87 percent of the stock. The 10 largest institutional investors owned 22.50 percent of the stock; the five largest, 13.8 percent.

E.W. Scripps

Ten Largest Institutional Investors, 1999

Institution	Type	Shares Owned	% of Total Shares
Wellington Management	MM	2,190,850	3.87%
Oak Valley Capital Mgt	MM	1,692,711	2.86
Mutual Shares	MF	1,477,500	2.50
Fleming R Hld	MM	1,382,010	2.34
Tudor Investment	MM	1,322,210	2.24
First Manhattan	MM	1,195,937	2.02
Mutual Qualified	MF	1,073,300	1.81
Mutual Beacon (USA)	MF	1,052,000	1.78
Gardner Investment	MM	980,228	1.66
Oak Value Fund	MF	845,135	1.43

Gannett Company

The Gannett Company was founded in 1906. It owns *USA Today*, which has a circulation of 2.2 million. As of 1999, the company also owned 74 dailies with a combined circulation of 6.7 million, and a variety of non-daily publications, including *USA Weekend*, a weekly magazine. The company also owned 21 television stations, a news service, and commercial printing companies. The newspaper segment accounted for 81.2 percent of the company's revenues; broadcasting accounted for 14.1 percent.

The Gannett Company went public in 1967. Shareholders of the common stock are entitled to one vote per share. The company's stock is widely held and voting power is not controlled by any single group.

Three members of the Gannett board have experience working in media. Two of these are officers in the company and the other was chairman and CEO of a company that merged with Gannett in 1986. Gannett's CEO and chairman has extensive journalistic experience.

Board members receive an annual fee of $45,000 plus $1,500 for each board meeting attended. Committee chairs receive an annual fee of $5,000, and each committee member receives $1,000 for each committee meeting attended.

The company is a diversified media company owning newspapers, broadcast stations and cable television systems. It also engages in marketing, commercial printing, data services and news programming. The newspaper operation is the company's major revenue source. 1998 marked the seventh year in a row that Gannett had record revenues and profits.

Advertising revenues accounted for 57.5 percent of the company's total revenues in 1998; circulation accounted for 19.7 percent of total revenues. Advertising revenues increased 11.7 percent between 1997 and 1998; circulation revenues increased 6.6 percent. Total revenues increased by 8.3 percent between 1997 and 1998.

Between 1988 and 1998, advertising revenues increased 54.2 percent; circulation revenues increased by 47.3 percent. Total revenues increased by 66 percent over the 11-year period. Net income increased by 174.4 percent over the same period. The company's operating profit margins were very stable over the 11-year period; with the exception of 1991, profit margins were in the mid to high 20 percent range. Return on shareholder's equity was also stable in the low to mid 20 percent range. Between 1992 and 1997, cumulative shareholder investment return for Gannett was 172 percent, higher than the S&P 500 (152 percent) and comparable to the S&P Publishing/Newspaper Index (179 percent). The price of a share of stock increased 247.1 percent between 1988 and 1997. The price-earnings ratio was 24 in 1997.

In 1999, there were 1,133 institutional investors owning 79.50 percent of the company's common stock. In 1998, 1,083 institutional investors owned 77.42 percent of the stock.

In 1999, mutual funds comprised 51.1 percent of the institutional investors, money managers 36.5 percent, banks 8.3 percent, insurance companies 3.8 percent, and colleges .3 percent. The University of California system, the largest institutional investor, owned 3.62 percent of the stock. The 10 largest institutional investors owned 22.11 percent of the shares; the five largest 14.24 percent.

Gannett

Ten Largest Institutional Investors, 1999

Institution	Type	Shares Owned	% of Total Shares
U of California	CO	10,099,500	3.62%
Barclays Bank	BA	9,104,252	3.26
Tukman Capital	MM	8,859,300	3.17
Mellon Bank	BA	6,118,358	2.19
Invs Capital Management	MM	5,592,636	2.00
Bank of Ireland	MM	4,932,855	1.77
Bankers Trust N.Y.	BA	4,560,940	1.63
Equitable Cos.	IN	4,328,865	1.55
IDS New Dimensions	MF	4,200,000	1.50
Vanguard Windsor II Fund	MF	3,959,900	1.42

Gray Communications Systems

As of 1999, Gray Communications Systems owned three daily newspapers with a total circulation of 107,000, and one weekly shopper. The company also owned 10 network-affiliated television stations, paging operations and a satellite uplink business.

Gray Communications went public in 1995 and has two classes of stock. Class A shareholders have 10 votes per share; Class B one vote per share. Bull Run Corporation owns 17 percent of Class A shares, representing 27.6 percent of the voting interest. Parties affiliated with Bull Run own an additional 12.7 percent of Class A stock, representing an additional 21 percent of the voting interest in Gray Communications.

No member of the nine-person Gray Communications Systems board has experience working in media companies. None has journalistic experience. Representatives of Bull Run Corporation, which effectively owns the company, dominate the board.

Non-employee members of the board receive an annual fee of $12,000. They also receive $1,000 for each board and committee meeting attended. The board chairman receives $18,000 annually and $1,200 per meeting, while committee chairmen also receive $1,200 per meeting. Non-employee members receive an annual option to purchase up to 7,500 shares of Class B common stock at a price per share equal to the market price at the time of the option. The options are exercisable until the end of the first month following the close of the company's fiscal year.

Broadcasting accounted for 70.6 percent of the company's revenues in 1998; newspaper publishing accounted for 22.8 percent. Newspaper advertising revenues increased 20.7% between 1997 and 1998 and accounted for 18.1 percent of the company's total revenues. Circulation revenues increased 11.2 percent from 1997 to 1998 and accounted for 4.1% of total revenues. Broadcast revenues increased 25.9 percent from 1997 to 1998. Newspaper publishing revenues increased 19.5 percent over the same period. Total revenues increased 24.5 percent.

Between 1994 and 1998, newspaper advertising revenues increased 118.7 percent; circulation revenues by 102.2 percent. Total revenues increased by 119.9 percent between 1995 and 1997. Operating profit margins have remained stable the last three years at about 20 percent.

Between 1992 and 1997, cumulative shareholder investment return for Gray Communication was 229 percent, exceeding both the NYSE Market Index (129 percent) and the NYSE Television Broadcasting Stations Industry Index (75.9 percent).

In 1999, 39 institutional investors owned 20.54 percent of the company's common stock. This compares to 41 institutional investors owning 19.85 percent of the stock in 1998.

Mutual funds represented 61.5 percent of the institutional investors, money managers 28.2 percent, and banks 10.3 percent. The largest institutional investor, Goldman Sachs, owned 4.22 percent of the shares. The 10 largest institutional investors owned 15.14 percent of the company's stock, the five largest, 11.44 percent.

Gray Communications

Ten Largest Institutional Investors, 1999

Institution	Type	Shares Owned	% of Total Shares
Goldman Sachs & Company	MM	288,600	4.22%
Citifunds Small Cap Growth	MF	159,045	2.33
Barclays Bank	BA	128,085	1.87
Gamco Investors	MM	127,200	1.86
Div In Spec Equ	MF	78,550	1.15
Managers Funds SpecialEquity Fund	MF	67,500	.99
Entrp Acc Sm-Cp	MF	52,500	.77
Citisel-400	MF	50,700	.74
Dimmesn Fund Adv	MM	45,050	.66
Gabel Equitable Trust	MF	37,500	.55

Hollinger International

As of 1999, the Hollinger Company directly owned three daily newspapers in the United States, including the *Chicago-Sun Times*. It also owned 78 non-daily newspapers and the Community Group, which consists of 166 newspapers and related publications. The company's total of 54 daily newspapers had a combined circulation of 1.1 million. Its 108 non-daily newspapers had a combined circulation of 1.5 million. Its 79 free publications had a circulation of 1.5 million. For accounting and management purposes, the *Jerusalem Post* is included in the Community Group.

Hollinger International is controlled by Hollinger Inc., which owns a controlling block of Hollinger International's stock. Hollinger International went public in 1994 with two classes of common stock. Class A shareholders are entitled to one vote per share; Class B shareholders are entitled to 10 votes per share. Class B shares are held directly or indirectly by Hollinger Inc., which is controlled by its chairman and chief executive officer, Conrad M. Black.

Hollinger International's 16-person board of directors is composed of members who represent a wide range of businesses and institutions. Five members of the board are former high-ranking government officials, including former Secretary of State Henry A. Kissinger and the former governor of Illinois, James R. Thompson. Other board members are from industry (Archer-Daniels-Midland, Aurec Ltd, Sotheby's Holdings, Weidenfeld & Nicolson and The Limited). The former editor of the *Toronto Sun*, Barbara Amiel Black, is on the board. Four members of the board have experience working in media companies. With the exception of Barbara Amiel Black, none of the board members appears to have experience in journalism.

Directors receive an annual fee of $27,500 and a fee of $2,000 for each board or committee meeting attended.

The company's business is concentrated in the publication of newspapers in the United States, Canada, the United Kingdom and Israel. Its revenues are derived principally from advertising, circulation and, to a lesser extent, job printing. Approximately 27 percent of the company's operating revenues come from its U.S. newspaper group.

Advertising accounted for 70.7 percent of its U.S. group's revenues; circulation for 22.4 percent of revenues. Advertising revenues declined 3.9 percent from 1997 to 1998; circulation revenues dropped 11.5 percent. Total revenues declined .7 percent from 1997 to 1998.

Between 1995 and 1998, advertising revenues increased 11.9 percent and circulation revenues increased by 1.8 percent. Total revenues increased 142.6 percent over the four-year period and net income was up 90.1 percent. Operating profit margins increased from 8.3 percent to 12.8 percent over the same period.

Cumulative shareholder investment return on Hollinger International stock was 12.4 percent between 1994 and 1997. This is significantly lower than the cumulative shareholder return for the NSYE Market Index (108 percent) and the Media General Industry Group Index (89.8 percent). The price-earnings ratio was 11 in 1997.

Institutional ownership increased from 48.43 percent in 1998 to 62.67 percent in 1999. The number of institutional investors increased from 171 to 226.

In 1999, mutual funds represented 51.8 percent of the institutional investors; money managers 41.2 percent, banks 5.8 percent, and insurance companies, 1.3 percent. BankAmerica, the largest institutional investor, owned 3.82 percent of the stock. The 10 largest institutional investors owned 25.27 percent of the stock; the five largest, 15.64 percent.

Hollinger International

Ten Largest Institutional Investors, 1999

Institution	Type	Shares Owned	% of Total Shares
BankAmerica	BA	3,609,680	3.82%
Pimco Advsrs LP	MM	3,495,489	3.70
Bankers Trust N.Y.	BA	2,731,676	2.89
Banc One Corp	BA	2,573,613	2.72
Moody, Aldrich	MM	2,372,730	2.51
Global Strategy Financial	MM	2,144,900	2.27
Mellon Bank	BA	2,043,934	2.16
Barclays Bank	BA	1,998,597	2.11
Citigroup Inc	MM	1,947,377	2.06
State Street Research High Income	MF	1,918,000	1.03

The Journal Register Company

The Journal Register Company was formed in 1990 and completed its initial public offering in 1997. As of 1999, the company owned 24 daily newspapers and 185 non-daily publications.[97] Daily newspaper circulation was 652,000 and non-daily circulation was about 3.7 million. The company also owned

---

[97] In March of 2000, the Journal Register announced its intention to sell its Midwestern newspapers, leaving it with 20 dailies and 143 nondaily newspapers. The reason given for selling the papers was to lift the price of the company's stock. Lucia Moses, *Journal Register sheds papers in wake of Thomson sell-off*, Editor & Publisher, March 6, 2000, p. 14.

four commercial printing operations and a company that develops software for the newspaper industry.

Holders of the common stock are entitled to one vote per share. Warburg, Pincus Capital Company owns 50.1 percent of the stock, and thus voting control of the company.

Representatives of E.M. Warburg, Pincus & Company dominate the seven-person Journal Register board, occupying three of the seven seats. Three of the board members have experience working for a media company. None of the board members appears to have experience in journalism.

Non-employee directors receive an annual fee of $10,000 and $1,000 for each board meeting attended. Non-employee members also receive a non-qualified stock option to purchase 10,000 shares of common stock annually.

Substantially all of the Journal Register Company's revenues relate to newspaper publishing. In 1998, the company had record revenues and EBITDA. Advertising accounted for 73.3 percent of 1998 revenues, circulation for 20.9 and commercial printing 5.7 percent. Advertising revenues increased 17.2 percent from 1997 to 1998 and circulation revenues increased 11.4%. Total revenues were up 18.8 percent.

Between 1993 and 1998, advertising revenues increased 55 percent; circulation revenues 53.5 percent. Total revenues increased 57 percent over the five-year period. With the exception of its first year as a publicly traded company, operating profit margins have been in the mid to high 20 percent range.

The Journal Register completed an initial public offering in May 1997 and began trading on the New York Stock Exchange in May 1998. The Warburg, Pincus group of companies, together, owned approximately 75 percent of the company's outstanding shares. The stock has traded between $14 and $21. The price-earnings ratio was 37 in 1999.

In 1999, there were 88 institutional investors owning 21.04 percent of the stock not owned by Warburg, Pincus. In 1998, there were 80 institutional investors owning 19.35 percent of the stock.

In 1999, mutual funds represented 50 percent of the institutional investors, money managers 38.4 percent, banks 9.3

percent, and insurance companies 23 percent. New South Capital, the largest institutional investor, owned 2.75 percent of the stock. The 10 largest institutional investors owned 13.66 percent of the shares, the five largest 9.78 percent.

Journal Register

Ten Largest Institutional Investors, 1999

Institution	Type	Shares Owned	% of Total Shares
New South Capital	MM	1,298,950	2.75%
Cambiar Inv	MM	1,054,450	2.23
Fidelity Low Price	MF	947,700	2.00
Trinity Cap Jck	MM	710,000	1.50
Selig Frontier	MF	616,300	1.30
Avenir Corp	MM	427,800	.90
Morgan JP & Co.	BA	394,500	.83
High Rock Capital	MM	350,400	.74
Seligman Henderson Global	MF	341,000	.72
N&B	MM	320,834	.68

Knight Ridder, Inc.

Knight Ridder resulted from the 1974 merger of Knight Newspapers and Ridder Publications, each of which had been public companies since 1969. In 1999, the Knight Ridder Company owned 31 daily newspapers with a combined circulation of 3.9 million and 21 non-daily newspapers with a combined circulation 9.2 million. It was also a partner in two newsprint mills.

The company's stock is widely held. Owners of common stock are entitled to one vote per share. In 1997, the company issued Series B Preferred Stock in connection with its purchase of newspapers owned by the Disney Company. Disney owns nearly all of the preferred stock and is entitled to two votes per share, giving Disney about 4 percent of the voting power.

Two members of the 11-person Knight Ridder board have experience working in newspaper companies; one has journalistic experience.

Non-employee members of the board receive an annual retainer of $30,000, plus $1,500 for each board meeting and $1,000 for each committee meeting attended. Half of the retainer is paid in company stock. A director may choose to receive the balance of the retainer in company stock. Each non-employee director also receives an annual grant of options to purchase 2,000 shares of stock.

Advertising accounted for 76.4 percent of company revenues in 1998; circulation for 19 percent. From 1997 to 1998, advertising revenues increased 7.3 percent and circulation revenues by 3.5 percent. Total revenues increased 7.5 percent from 1997 to 1998.

Between 1988 and 1998, advertising revenues increased 55.1 percent and circulation revenues increased 58.4 percent. Total revenues increased 60.7 percent over the same time period. The company's net income increased by 133.9 percent over the 11-year period. Net income as a percent of total revenues hovered in the mid to low teens during most of this time, rising to 16.3 percent in 1998. Operating margins did not grow during most of this time period, but return on stockholder's equity increased substantially the past three years, reaching 30.8 percent in 1997 and dropping back to 22.8 percent in 1998.

Between 1992 and 1997, Knight Ridder's cumulative shareholder investment return of 101 percent was below that of the S&P 500 (152 percent) and the S&P Publishing/Newspaper Index (162 percent). The price of a share of the company's stock increased 121.2 percent between 1988 and 1997. The price-earnings ratio in 1997 was 21.8.

A total of 553 institutional investors owned 84.77 percent of the company's stock in 1999. In 1998, 454 institutional investors owned 88.3 percent of the stock.

Mutual funds represented 54.4 percent of the institutional investors, money managers 34.7 percent, banks 7.1 percent, insurance companies 3.6 percent, and colleges .2 percent. Southeast Asset Management, the largest institutional investor, owned 8.58 percent of the stock. The 10 largest institutional investors owned 37.26 percent of the company's stock; the five largest, 26.16 percent. The two largest institutional investors owned 16.53 percent.

Knight Ridder

Ten Largest Institutional Investors, 1999

Institution	Type	Shares Owned	% of Total Shares
So'E Asset	MM	6,760,898	8.58%
Oakmark Fund	MF	6,266,100	7.95
Longleaf Partners	MF	3,150,000	4.00
Harris Association	MM	2,224,188	2.81
Barclays Bank	BA	2,216,416	2.81
T. Rowe Price Equity Inc	MF	2,100,000	2.66
Mellon Bank	BA	1,949,409	2.47
Aeltus Investment Mgt	MM	1,810,527	2.30
Chase Manhattan	BA	1,503,138	1.91
Aetna V-Growth & Income	MF	1,386,400	1.76

Lee Enterprises

Lee Enterprises was founded in 1890 and went public in 1969. As of 1999, the company owned 21 daily newspapers with a circulation of 623,000. It also owned 11 weekly newspapers with a combined circulation of 66,800, 41 classified publications with a non-paid circulation of 1.7 million, and other specialty publications. The company owned nine television stations.[98]

The company has two classes of stock. Shareholders of common stock have one vote per share; Class B common stock shareholders have 10 votes per share. The transfer of Class B common stock is restricted. This stock was issued to stockholders of record in 1986 and is converted at sale or at the option of the holder into common stock.

There are 12 members of the Lee Enterprises board of directors. Five members of the board, three of whom are officers in the company, have experience working for media companies. One of these has experience working as a journalist.

Non-employee directors receive a $24,400 annual retainer and $1,000 for each board meeting attended and $700 for each committee meeting attended. Non-employee members of the board receive an annual grant of 500 shares of common stock and may elect to receive 50 percent of the cash retainer and meeting fees in common stock.

Lee has two principal businesses: publishing and broadcasting. The company had record earnings in 1998. Publishing accounted for 74 percent of 1998 revenues, broadcasting for 24.4 percent. Newspaper advertising revenues increased 8.9 percent from 1997 to 1998 and accounted for 37.9 percent of 1998 revenues. Circulation revenues increased 1.7 percent and accounted for 15.8 percent of revenues. Total revenues increased 15.8 percent between 1997 and 1998.

---

[98] The company announced in March 2000 that it intends to sell its broadcasting segment in order to focus on its core publishing and on-line business, *Lee: Bye-bye, Broadcast!*, Editor & Publisher, March 6, 2000, pp. 3-4.

Newspaper advertising revenues increased 84 percent between 1988 and 1998; circulation revenues by 73.1 percent. Revenues increased by 104.8 percent and net income by 52.1 percent. Between 1988 and 1998, newspaper operating margins were steady in the mid to high 20 percent range, hitting a high of 27.9 percent in 1997. Operating profit margins for both the publishing segment and the broadcasting operations combined were steady in the mid to low 20 percent range over the 11-year period.

Cumulative stockholder investment return for Lee Enterprises was below both the S&P 500 and the S&P Publishing/Newspaper Index. Between 1992 and 1997, Lee stockholders' cumulative return was 99.2 percent, compared with 157 percent for the S&P 500 and 148 percent for the S&P Publishing/Newspaper Index. The price of the company's stock remained flat between 1988 and 1997. The price-earnings ratio was 23 in 1997.

A total of 196 institutional investors owned 68.26 percent of the company's common stock in 1999. This compares to 177 institutional investors owning 64.3 percent of the stock in 1998.

In 1999, money managers accounted for 44.9 percent of the institutional investors, mutual funds for 37.2 percent, banks 14.8 percent, insurance companies 2.6 percent, and colleges .5 percent. Ariel Capital Management was the largest institutional investor, owning 10.95 percent of the publicly traded shares.

The 10 largest institutional investors owned 36.64 percent of the common stock; the five largest, 28.81 percent. The two largest institutional investors owned 21.43 percent.

Lee Enterprises

Ten Largest Institutional Investors, 1999

Institution	Type	Shares Owned	% of Total Shares
Ariel Capital Management	MM	3,590,215	10.95%
Harris Assoc.	MM	3,435,884	10.48
Babson (DL) & Co	MM	888,788	2.71
U.S. Bancorp (MN)	BA	790,920	2.41
Barclays Bank	BA	737,488	2.25
Gamco Investors	MM	713,100	2.18
Harris Everett	MM	493,780	1.51
Lasalle National Trust	BA	480,138	1.46
Delphi Management	MM	440,650	1.34
CREF-Stock	MF	436,800	1.33

The McClatchy Company

The McClatchy Company dates to the California Gold Rush era of 1857, when James McClatchy founded the *Sacramento Bee*. The company diversified into radio and television in the 1970's, but has since sold those holdings. As of 1999, the company owned 11 daily newspapers with a combined circulation of 1.4 million. It also owned 12 non-daily newspapers with an average circulation of 65,000. In addition, it owned an online publishing company and was a part owner of a newsprint mill.

The McClatchy Company went public in 1988. The McClatchy family retains control of the company. The company has two classes of stock. Class A is publicly traded, and shareholders elect four Class A members of the board of directors. On all other matters, Class A shareholders have a one-tenth vote for each share owned. Class B shareholders are members of the McClatchy family.

They are entitled to one vote per share and elect nine Class B members of the board of directors. Class B shareholders are party to an agreement that permits the transfer of any shares of Class B stock only to current owners of Class B stock, to any lineal descendent of Charles K. McClatchy, or to a trust for the exclusive benefit of a lineal descendent of Charles K. McClatchy. The agreement terminates in the year 2047.

There are 13 members on the McClatchy board. Four are Class A directors and nine are Class B directors. The board is dominated by members of the McClatchy family (four) and by trustees (three) of various McClatchy family trusts. At least two of the family members have experience working in journalism. Another outside board member, Larry Jinks, has significant journalistic experience.

Non-employee members of the board receive $30,000 per year plus $1,200 per day for meetings of the board of directors and $1,000 per day for attending committee meetings. The Chair receives an additional $50,000. Each non-employee member receives an option of 2,500 shares of Class A stock annually.

Almost all of McClatchy's income comes from its newspapers. The non-newspaper operations account for 1.8 percent of total company revenues. Of the newspaper revenue, 78.1 percent comes from advertising and 16.8 percent from circulation. Advertising revenues increased 49.8 percent from 1997 to 1998; circulation revenue increased 51.4 percent. These increases reflect the acquisition of the Minneapolis *Star Tribune* in 1998. Between 1988 and 1998, the company's advertising revenue increased by 166.7 percent and circulation revenue increased 181.6 percent.

Between 1988 and 1997, the company's net income increased by 112.3 percent. The company's operating profit margin increased by 33.4 percent from 14 percent to 18.6 percent over the same time period and that growth occurred in the past two years. Otherwise, profit margins hovered around the 14 percent range.

Between 1992 and 1997, cumulative shareholder investment return for the McClatchy Company was 92.4 percent. This compares to 127 percent for the S&P Mid Cap 400 Index and 150 percent for the company's peer group, which is composed of comparable newspaper companies. Between 1993 and 1997, the price of a share of stock increased 43.9 percent. The 1997 price-earnings ratio was 18.

A large increase of institutional ownership occurred from 1998 to 1999. In 1998, 118 institutional investors owned 67.26 percent of the company's publicly traded stock; in 1999, 147 owned 81.12 percent.

Mutual funds comprised 45.6 percent of the institutional investors, money managers 42.9 percent, banks 10.2 percent, and insurance companies 1.4 percent. Wellington Management, the largest institutional investor, owned 8.2 percent of the stock. The 10 largest institutional investors owned 42.63 percent of the company's stock; the five largest, 29.97 percent. The two largest owned 16.24 percent.

McClatchy Company

Ten Largest Institutional Investors, 1999

Institution	Type	Shares Owned	% of Total Shares
Wellington Management	MM	1,323,050	8.20%
Private Cap Management	MM	1,296,425	8.04
Vanguard Prime Cap Fund	MF	1,000,000	6.20
Gamco Investors	MM	749,657	4.65
U.S. Bancorp (MN)	BA	464,278	2.88
Pitcairn Group	MM	453,307	2.81
Barclays Bank	BA	422,029	2.62
Delphi Management	MM	421,624	2.61
Goldman Sachs & Company	MM	373,368	2.32
First Pacific Advisors	MM	371,225	2.30

Media General, Inc.

The Media General Company was founded in 1879 and went public as Richmond Newspapers, Inc., in 1966. Richmond Newspapers, Inc., created Media General as a holding company in 1969. In 1999, the company owned 21 daily and nearly 100 weekly newspapers and periodicals. Daily newspaper circulation was approximately 840,000. The company owned a 40 percent stake in the *Denver Post*, with a circulation of 337,000. The company owned 14 network-affiliated television stations. It also owned two cable systems, a cable advertising firm, and an interest in a cable advertising interconnect business serving five cable systems in the Washington, D.C., area. It also owned a newsprint mill and had part interest in a second mill. Its publishing segment accounts for 53 percent of it revenues; broadcasting accounts for 18 percent.

The company has two classes of stock. Class A shareholders elect 30 percent of the board of directors; Class B shareholders elect 70 percent. The Bryan family controls a majority of Class B stock.

The Media General board of directors is composed of nine members. Three have experience working for media companies; two have significant journalistic experience.

Non-employee members of the board receive 50 percent of the $55,000 annual compensation in deferred Class A stock units. Directors may opt to receive the other 50 percent in cash or deferred stock units.

The company is a diversified media company, but newspaper publishing remains its core business. In 1998, the company had record revenues, profits, and cash flow. Publishing accounted for 53.2 percent of 1998 revenues, broadcasting accounted for 17.5 percent, cable television for 16.1 percent and newsprint for 13.1 percent.

The company does not provide a breakdown of advertising and circulation revenues, but it did provide the following narrative:

> Excluding acquisitions and dispositions, Publishing Segment revenues improved $22 million (5%) in 1998 over 1997. At the Company's three largest daily metropolitan newspapers,

revenues rose $14.4 million as a result of expanded lineage (up 2.4%) and higher advertising rates (up 2.9%). This increase was principally the result of strong performance in classified advertising (led by the employment category) and retail advertising (driven by preprints). Additionally, the Company's Virginia and North Carolina community newspapers produced a revenue increase of $5 million over the prior year, due to solid classified advertising.

Revenues for the publishing segment increased 6.7 percent from 1997 to 1998. Total revenues were up 7 percent. Between 1988 and 1998, the company revenues increased 63.7 percent. Operating profit margins showed a steady increase from 1988 (2.1 percent), hitting a high of 16 percent in 1998.

Media General is one of the companies that does not compare its cumulative rate of shareholder investment return to the S&P 500, choosing, instead, to compare it with the AMEX Composite Index. Cumulative shareholder return for Media General exceeded the AMEX Composite Index, but was lower than the S&P Publishing Index for 1992 to 1997. Cumulative shareholder return for Media General was 160 percent, the AMEX, 71.8 percent and the S&P Publishing Index, 179 percent. The price of a share of the company's stock increased 140.6 percent between 1988 and 1997. It price-earnings ratio was 18 in 1997.

In 1999, 230 institutional investors owned 64.82 percent of the company's common stock; in 1998, 186 institutional investors owned 64.79 percent.

In 1999, mutual funds represented 47 percent of the institutional investors; money managers 42.2 percent, banks 8.7 percent, insurance companies 1.7 percent, and colleges .4 percent. Gamco Investors, the largest institutional investor, owned 12.58 percent of the stock. The 10 largest institutional investors owned 34.51 percent of the company's stock; the five largest, 26.6 percent.

Media General

Ten Largest Institutional Investors, 1999

Institution	Type	Shares Owned	% of Total Shares
Gamco Investors	MM	3,310,100	12.58%
Gabelli Value Fund	MF	1,678,000	6.38
Cap Guardian Trust	MM	745,700	2.83
Am Var In-Gr-In	MF	636,100	2.42
Barclays Bank	BA	630,737	2.40
Mutual Shares	MF	520,200	1.98
Davenport & Co.	MM	410,924	1.56
Mellon Bank	BA	404,909	1.54
King Investment Adv	MM	402,200	1.53
Gabel Equity Trust Inc	MF	345,000	1.31

The New York Times Company

As of 1999, the New York Times Company owned 20 newspapers, including the *New York Times* and the *Boston Globe*, with a total daily circulation of 2.3 million and a Sunday circulation of 3.2 million. The company owned eight television and two radio stations. It also owned golfing magazines, a part interest in forest-product ventures, and had a 50 percent interest in the *International Herald Tribune*. The newspaper publishing segment accounted for 91 percent of total revenues.

The company went public in 1967. It has two classes of stock. Owners of Class A common stock have limited voting rights and elect five of the 15 members of the board of directors. Class B shareholders elect the other 10 members of the board and are entitled to vote on all matters presented to the shareholders. Class B stock is controlled by a family trust (the "1997 Trust").

Of the 15 members of the Times Company board, four are family members, three of whom have experience working in journalism. No other member of the board has journalism experience.

Non-employee board members receive an annual retainer of $25,000 and $1,000 for attending each board meeting. Each non-employee board member receives an annual option to purchase 4,000 shares of the company's Class A stock. (The Times stock split 2-1 on June 17, 1998.)

The New York Times Company is a diversified media company, but newspaper publishing is its core business. In 1998, the company had record earnings, cash flow, and revenues. In 1998, newspaper publishing accounted for 90.7 percent of its revenues, magazine publishing for 4.1 percent and broadcasting for 5.1 percent.

Newspaper advertising revenues increased 5.5 percent from 1997 to 1998 and accounted for 63 percent of the company's revenues. Circulation revenues were up 1.8 percent between 1997 and 1998 and accounted for 22.2 percent of the company's revenues. Total revenues in 1998 increased 1.7 percent over 1997.

Advertising revenue increased 47.5 percent between 1991 and 1998; circulation revenue increased by 66.9 percent. The company's revenues increased 69.1 percent between 1991 and 1998. Profit margins were in the mid single digits in the early 1990s, climbing to 15.9 percent in 1997 and 17.5 percent in 1998. Return on shareholder's equity followed a similar pattern, in the low single digits in the early 1990's, climbing to 15 percent in 1997 and 17 percent in 1998.

Between 1992 and 1997, return on shareholders investment in the New York Times exceeded both the S&P 500 and the company's peer group, which is composed of comparable communication companies. Cumulative shareholder return was 176 percent, compared with 151 percent for the S&P 500 and 165 percent for the peer group. The price of the company's stock increased 140.2 percent between 1988 and 1997. The price-earnings ratio was 22.

In 1999, 678 institutional investors owned 62.08 percent of the New York Times Company's publicly traded shares. This compares to 635 institutional investors owning 68.18 percent of the stock in 1988.

In 1999, mutual funds made up 59 percent of the institutional investors; money managers 31.9 percent, banks 5.6 percent, insurance companies 3.2 percent, and colleges 0.2 percent. The largest institutional investor, Barclays Bank, owned 3.02 percent of the shares. The 10 largest institutional investors owned 18.85 percent; the 5 largest, 11.4 percent.

New York Times Company

Ten Largest Institutional Investors, 1999

Institution	Type	Shares Owned	% of Total Shares
Barclays Bank	BA	5,406,145	3.02%
Mellon Bank	BA	4,530,001	2.53
Lazard Freres	MM	4,150,630	2.32
Goldman Sachs & Company	MM	3,157,124	1.76
Morgan JP & Co.	BA	3,156,050	1.76
Bankers Trust	BA	2,824,267	1.58
Aeltus Investment Management	MM	2,819,719	1.58
State Street Corporation	MM	2,752,978	1.54
Aetna Variable-Growth & Income	MF	2,609,800	1.46
Boston Partners	MM	2,314,400	1.29

The Pulitzer Publishing Company

The Pulitzer Company was founded in 1878 by Joseph Pulitzer, and has operated continuously under the direction of the Pulitzer family. In 1999, it owned 14 newspapers with a total circulation of 581,000. Two of its newspapers, *The* (Tucson) *Star* and the *St. Louis Post-Dispatch*, accounted for 72.5 percent of company circulation. The remaining 12 newspapers had a combined circulation of 159,000. In 1998, the company spun off its nine network-affiliated television stations and five radio stations to Hearst-Argyle. The company also had an interest in the Arizona Diamondbacks and St. Louis Cardinals baseball teams.

Pulitzer went public in 1986 after a hostile takeover attempt by some members of the Pulitzer family. The company has two classes of stock. Holders of the common stock are entitled to one vote per share; holders of the Class B common stock are entitled to 10 votes per share. Shares of the outstanding Class B common stock, representing 89.55 percent of the combined voting power, are held by a voting trust (the "Voting Trust"). The trustees are members of the Pulitzer family.

Pulitzer has a nine-person board of directors. Compensation of non-employee directors is $5,000 per year plus $750 per meeting. Options to purchase 3,000 shares of common stock are automatically granted to each non-employee director annually.

In 1998, the company restructured, selling its television stations. In 1999, eighty-two institutional investors owned 35.68 percent of the company's common stock. Mutual funds accounted for 70.7 percent of the institutional investors, money managers 25.6 percent, banks 2.4 percent, and insurance companies 1.2 percent. The 10 largest institutional investors owned 24.91 percent of the common stock; and the five largest, 17.45 percent.

Pulitzer

Ten Largest Institutional Investors, 1998

Institution	Type	Shares Owned	% of Total Shares
Nicholas Fund	MF	470,866	6.63%
Oak Valley Capital Mgt	MF	264,353	3.72
Mutual Qualified	MF	172,000	2.42
Avenir Corporation	MM	167,100	2.35
JGD Management	MM	164,800	2.32
Sogen International Fund	MF	140,000	1.97
Caxton Associates	MM	139,990	1.97
Fidelity Low Price	MF	100,000	1.41
Fasciano Mich F	MM	80,000	1.13
Massachusetts Investors Growth	MF	70,000	.99

The Times Mirror Company

Over the last few years, the Times Mirror Company has been restructuring, recapitalizing and overhauling its operations. The "old" Times Mirror Company has been replaced with the "new" Times Mirror Company. As of 1999, the company owned seven dailies and had a 50% interest in a Spanish-language daily published in Southern California. Total daily circulation was 2.4 million; Sunday circulation was 3.1 million. In 1998, the company acquired 24 alternative classified publications in Southern California. The company owned a number of specialty consumer magazines. It sold its cable operations in 1995. In early 2000, the company agreed to be acquired by the Tribune Company.

Holders of Series A common stock are entitled to one vote per share and holders of Series C are entitled to 10 votes per share. The Chandler trusts control nearly all of the Series C stock. FMR Corporation owns 15.6 percent of the Series A stock.

There are 14 members on the Times Mirror board of directors. The Chandler family is heavily represented through family membership (three) and membership of trustees (three) of the various Chandler trusts. None of the board members appears to have any experience in journalism.

Non-employee members of the board receive an annual retainer of 500 shares of Series A common stock. In addition, each receives a cash payment equal to the value of 500 shares. Committee chairs receive 60 shares of Series A and a cash payment equal to the value of 60 shares of Series A. Non-employee members also receive an annual option grant for 5,000 share of Series A common stock

Newspaper publishing is the company's core business, accounting for 76.7 percent of 1998 revenues, up from 75.6 percent in 1997. Newspaper advertising revenues increased 6.2 percent between 1997 and 1998 and accounted for 59.4 percent of the company's revenues. Circulation revenues were down .2 percent and accounted for 14.4 percent of the company's revenues. Total revenues were up 4.5 percent from 1997 to 1998.

Newspaper advertising revenues were relatively flat between 1988 and 1998, increasing only 9.7 percent. Circulation revenue increased 17.7 percent over the 11-year period. Total revenues dropped 11.9 percent between 1989 and 1998. Operating profit margins fell into the high single digits in the early 1990's, increasing to a 13.9 percent in 1997 before dropping to 7.1 percent in 1998.

Return on shareholders' investment in Times Mirror significantly outperformed the S&P 500 and the company's peer group, which is composed of comparable newspaper companies. Cumulative total shareholder return was 219 percent between 1992 and 1997, compared to 152 percent for the S&P 500 and 167 percent for the peer group. The price of the company's Series A common stock increased 160 percent between 1988 and 1997. The price-earnings ratio was 23 in 1997.

In 1999, 431 institutional investors owned 61.7 percent of the company's Series A common stock. In 1998, 418 institutional investors owned 63.58 percent of the stock.

In 1999, mutual funds accounted for 53.4 percent of the institutional investors, money managers 33.4 percent, banks 9.2 percent, insurance companies 3.5 percent, and colleges .5 percent. The largest institutional investor, Putnam Growth and Income, owned 7.63 percent of the stock. The 10 largest institutional investors owned 29.95 percent of the stock; the five largest, 21.26 percent.

Times Mirror

Ten Largest Institutional Investors, 1999

Institution	Type	Shares Owned	% of Total Shares
Putnam Growth & Income	MF	3,625,000	7.63%
Barclays Bank	BA	2,237,247	4.71
Fidelity Growth & Income	MF	2,128,100	4.48
Morgan JP & Co	BA	1,061,950	2.23
Bankers Trust N.Y.	BA	1,052,508	2.21
State Street Corp	MM	965,490	2.03
Putnam Vista-Growth & Income	MF	920,000	1.94
Oakmark Select Fund	MF	900,000	1.89
Fidelity Magellan Fund	MF	697,300	1.47
Vanguard Index 500	MF	644,728	1.36

The Tribune Company

The Tribune Company was founded in 1847. As of 1999,[99] it owned four newspapers, the most prominent of which is *The Chicago Tribune*, with a combined daily circulation of 1.3 million and a Sunday circulation of 1.9 million. The publishing segment generated about 50 percent of the company's operating revenues in 1998. The company owned 19 television and four radio stations. It was also involved in syndication activities, advertising placement services, cable-television programming, Internet and online-related business activities. The company also owned the Chicago Cubs baseball team and an entertainment company that develops and distributes television programming. Its education segment publishes books and educational material.

The company went public in 1983. Holders of the common stock are entitled to one vote per share; holders of Series B Convertible Preferred Stock are entitled to 9.16 votes per share. The Robert R. McCormick Tribune Foundation controls 18.37 percent of the common stock. The Northern Trust Company, which manages the company's ESOP, controls 100 percent of the preferred stock.

There are 12 members of the board of directors. Four have experience in journalism, two of whom are outside directors. Another board member is president of a major broadcasting company.

Non-employee board members receive annual stock awards, stock options and meeting fees. Certain committee chairs receive a supplemental stock award. Beginning in 1998, the basic stock award is determined by dividing $50,000 ($6,000 for the supplemental stock awards) by the fair market value of the common stock on the day of the annual meeting. On the date of each annual meeting, each non-employee director is also granted an option to purchase 2,000 shares of Tribune common stock at the fair market value that day. In addition, non-employee directors receive $1,500 for each board meeting attended and $1,000 for each committee meeting attended.

About half (50.3 percent) of the company's 1998 revenue

---

[99] In early 2000, the company entered into an agreement to purchase the Times Mirror Company.

came from publishing, with broadcasting accounting for 38.7 percent. In 1998, the company had record revenues, operating cash flow and EBITDA. Advertising revenue from the company's publishing segment increased 4.1 percent from 1997 to 1998 and accounted to 39 percent of total revenue. Circulation revenue dropped 2.7 percent from 1997 to 1998 and accounted for 8.2 percent of the total revenue. Total revenue was up 9.6 percent from 1997 to 1998.

Advertising revenue from the publishing segment increased 29.3 percent between 1988 and 1998; circulation revenue increased by 34 percent. Total revenue increased 45 percent over the 11-year period. Profit margins were in the mid to high teens through most of the 1990s, reaching 23.6% in both 1997 and 1998.

Stock market return on shareholder investment in the Tribune Company outperformed both the S&P 500 and the S&P Newspaper Publishing Group. Cumulative shareholder return was 182 percent between 1992 and 1997, compared with 151 percent for the S&P 500 and 162 percent for the S&P Newspaper Publishing Group. The price of a share of the company's stock has been relatively flat, increasing only 17.3 percent between 1988 and 1997. The price-earnings ratio was 25 in 1997.

A total of 693 institutional investors owned 59.89 percent of the company's shares in 1999. This compares to 650 institutional investors owning 58.89 percent of the shares in 1998.

In 1999, mutual funds represented 55.7 percent of the institutional investors, money managers 32.5 percent, banks 7.9 percent, insurance companies 3.8 percent, and colleges .1 percent. The largest institutional investor, John A. Levin, owed 3.48 percent of the stock. The 10 largest institutional investors owned 18.81 percent, the five largest, 11.86 percent.

Tribune Company

Ten Largest Institutional Investors, 1999

Institution	Type	Shares Owned	% of Total Shares
Levin (John A.)	MM	4,152,953	3.48%
Barclays Bank	BA	3,505,574	2.93
Bankers Trust N.Y.	BA	2,352,967	1.97
Scudder Kemper Investment	MM	2,153,510	1.80
Putnam Investment Mgt	MM	2,004,672	1.68
Inv Vo America	MF	1,953,200	1.63
Mellon Bank	BA	21,811,279	1.52
Equinox Capital	MM	1,551,800	1.30
State Street Corp	MM	1,491,697	1.25
Goldman Sachs & Company	MM	1,487,572	1.25

The Washington Post Company

The Washington Post Company owns two daily newspapers with a combined circulation of 830,000. It also owns the *Washington Post National Weekly Edition* with a circulation of 92,000, and the Gazette Newspapers–which publish one paid-circulation and 30 controlled-circulation weekly community newspapers with a total circulation of 443,000–and 50 percent of the *International Herald Tribune*. The company owns six network-affiliated television stations and 53 cable television systems. The company also publishes *Newsweek* and its several spin-off publications. The Post-Newsweek Business Information, Inc., subsidiary publishes trade periodicals and produces trade shows for the information-technology industry. The company also owns Kaplan Educational Centers, Inc. which prepares students to take standardized tests; Washingtonpost.Newsweek Interactive Company, which develops news and information products for electronic distribution; and Legi-Slate, Inc., a computerized database containing information on legislative and regulatory activities of the U.S. government.

The Washington Post Company went public in 1971 and has two classes of stock. Class A and B shareholders are entitled to one vote on matters on which each class of stock is entitled to vote. The company is controlled by the Graham family, who own nearly all of the Class A stock. Donald Graham has voting power over 34.5 percent of the Class B stock and the proxy to vote an additional 20 percent or so of the Class B shares owned by Berkshire Hathaway.

Two members of the controlling Graham family, as well as a trustee of the various family trusts, are on the 12-person Washington Post Company board. Five board members have experience in media companies, at least one of whom has experience in journalism.

Non-employee members of the board receive an annual fee of $40,000 and an additional $5,000 for service as chairman of a committee. The company reimburses directors for their expenses incurred in attending board and committee meetings.

The company is a diversified media company owning newspapers, broadcasting stations, cable systems, magazines and other related businesses. In 1998, newspapers accounted for 40.1 percent of revenues, with broadcasting and magazines providing 16.9 percent and 18.9 percent respectively. Cable provided another 14 percent of revenues.

The company does not provide a breakdown of revenues for its different operations. It did, however, provide the following in its 1998 10-K form:

> Newspaper division revenues increased 4 percent to $846.8 million from $812.9 million in 1997. Advertising revenues at the newspaper division rose 5 percent over the previous year. At *The Washington Post*, advertising revenues increased 4 percent as a result of higher rates and a slight increase in volume. Classified advertising revenues at *The*

Washington Post increased 5 percent primarily due to higher rates and higher recruitment volume. Retail advertising revenues at *The Post* declined 3 percent, primarily as a result of a 7.5 percent decline in inches. Other advertising revenues (including general and preprint) at *The Post* increased 11 percent; general advertising volume was essentially unchanged for 1998; however, preprint volume increased 6 percent.

The company does not provide a breakdown of circulation revenue. It did, however, provide the following narrative:

> Circulation revenues for the newspaper division remained essentially unchanged from 1997, with the extra week in 1998 offsetting the effects of a 1.3 percent decline in daily and Sunday circulation at *The Washington Post*.

Newspaper revenues increased 4.2 percent from 1997 to 1998; broadcasting revenues increased 5.7 percent. Total revenues increased by 7.9 percent. Between 1988 and 1996, net income actually declined, but increased by 48.2 percent from 1997 to 1998, largely due to the sale of properties. Between 1988 and 1998, profit margins remained stable in the mid-teens, ranging from a low of 14 percent (1991) to a high of 21.7 percent (1989). Return on stockholder's equity has been increasing over the period, reaching a high of 22.4 percent in 1997.

Between 1992 and 1997, cumulative shareholder investment return was lower than both the S&P 500 and the S&P Publishing Index. Cumulative shareholder return was 129 percent, compared with 152 percent for the S&P 500 and 179 percent for the S&P Publishing Index. The price-earnings ratio was 22 in 1997.

There are 292 institutional investors who owned 65.73 percent of the company's common stock in 1999. This compares to 270 institutions owning 62.52 percent of the stock in 1998.

In 1999 money managers represented 45.6 percent of the institutional investors, mutual funds 38.4 percent, banks 12.3 percent, insurance companies 3.4 percent, and colleges .3 percent. Berkshire

Hathaway, the largest institutional investor, owned 20.66 percent of the stock. The 10 largest institutional investors owned 41.03 percent of the shares; the five largest, 34.55 percent.

The Washington Post Company

Ten Largest Institutional Investors, 1999

Institution	Type	Shares Owned	% of Total Shares
Berkshire Hathw	IN	1,727,765	20.66%
Morgan JP &Co.	BA	656,335	7.85
Frnkl Resors	MM	192,354	2.30
Fleming(R) Hld	MM	175,137	2.09
Barclays Bank	BA	1137,107	1.64
Bankamerica	BA	132,974	1.59
Oak Valley Capital Mgt	MM	130,801	1.56
AIM Value Fnd	MF	124,000	1.48
Klingenstn, Flds	MM	77,582	.93
Bankers Trust N.Y.	BA	76,887	.92

Appendix B

Account of the June 1999 Mid-Year Media Review

by Gil Cranberg

There were several noteworthy things about the Mid-Year Media Review.

One was the attention paid to online investments. Spokesmen for *Tribune*, which gets the great bulk of revenue and profits from newspapers, barely mentioned the papers. All but Media General and Journal Register papers have websites. Lots of talk about hits and revenues from the sites, but virtually nothing about profits; it's clear that the investment isn't paying off now, but equally clear that almost all the companies regard their presence as essential to "protect the franchise" –that is, to keep others from stealing their classified ads by offering online classifieds. So much talk about the Internet I wondered at times if I walked into the wrong meeting. The analysts I talked to attributed the emphasis to the fact that newspapers are an old story and online is where growth will be.

Also noteworthy is how McClatchy and Washington Post were in a class by themselves by their disdain for short-term thinking. Donald Graham of the Post said bluntly that if you care about what the Post's next quarter's profits are, "sell the stock." He claimed not to even know quarterly results. He said the Post's "quirky attitude" toward quarters frees them to make certain long-term investments. Gary Pruitt of McClatchy likewise said he's never impressed by short-term results. Gannett people spoke immediately after Graham, and it was quite a contrast. They told the analysts they "won't be disappointed" with the consensus estimate for the third quarter of 86 cents a share. To be fair, though, even the New York Times spokesmen stressed quarterly results. Times Mirror said they're "absolutely focused on revenue and profit growth quarter by quarter.

Post, McClatchy and New York Times stood out in their emphasis that quality pays. Graham said that *The Post* is "strongly committed" to quality at the paper and online, "that we can't save our way to the future," that profits are strongly connected to quality and

The Post is "handsomely profitable." Pruitt said McClatchy's focus was on "journalistic excellence," that the way to reach higher circulation is to invest in quality. He was virtually the only one to talk about bigger newsholes to aid circulation growth. As for the *Times*, almost every word was either premium or quality, and frequently both were combined to describe the "high-value audience" they serve. They were upfront about saying the best way for them to grow is nationally where upscale readers will attract lucrative national ads, rather than in New York. CEO Russell Lewis said, "We have a continent to conquer" and their formula is "premium quality product equals good ad price." That, plus controlling costs aggressively. They didn't say this but I'm pretty sure the latter refers to their other papers, which never received mention.

Except for those three, talk about journalistic quality was scarce, though. Pulitzer's CEO, Robert Woodworth, did say, "Good journalism is good business." That said, however, no references were made to newshole or staffing in St. Louis, Pulitzer's flagship, and the company's VP for finance defined its franchise as "getting buyers and sellers together." As for Belo, usually described as having strong commitment to quality, its spokesman for *The Dallas Morning News*, former editor (now publisher) Burl Osborne, said not a word about the paper's quality, staffing, or newshole. Knight Ridder's Anthony Ridder said Knight Ridder people are always recognized as good journalists and now want to be recognized as good marketers. He paid special tribute to Mike Rogers, Vice President for Marketing, whose picture he flashed on a screen, the only Knight-Ridder executive so honored. A few of the executives–Robert Jelenic of Journal Register, Colleen Brown, in charge of broadcasting for Lee –boasted about news quality, but for the most part the media companies managed to discuss their operations without reference to the product itself. As for the analysts, none expressed interest in that aspect of the business. Questions from the floor touched on margins, FTEs (once), debt, circulation, and acquisition strategy, but nothing about what the companies actually produce for their customers.

Circulation clearly is a trouble spot. Several of the executives said as much. It was so troubling that a third of the companies avoided mention of it altogether and had to be asked from the floor.

Each time, the answer was "down" or "flat." Gannett termed circulation "a key area of concern."

Odds and ends: Many of the companies are flush with cash and looking for papers to buy. (Bad news, obviously, for remaining independents.) McClatchy is not in the market, as it has $900 million-plus debt after buying Minneapolis. Media General sold a cable system for $1.4 billion and paid $500 million in taxes, a source of much snickering by the analysts. Knight Ridder's "goal is to be industry leader fiscally." Central Newspapers kicked out several inside directors and now has 5-2 majority of outsiders. Their CEO called that "strengthening the board," the only reference to directors by anybody. Much talk, too much, about "one of best margins in the industry," EBITDA, and cost management.

Index

Advertising
    categories, 24-25
    dependence on, 24
    revenues, 24, 133
    newspapers transformed by, 107
    market segmentation and, 2, 9-10, 107, 116, 127, 131, 136, 140
    consumer preferences and, 140-141
American Journalism Review, 89, 90
American Society for Newspaper Editors
    statement of principles, 86
    credibility project, 5-6
Appert, Peter, 56-57, 58, 62
Arthur, Douglas, 57, 62

Baltimore Sun, 96
Bankers Trust, 45
Barclays Bank, 45
Barnes, Andrew, 97
A.H. Belo Corp., 4, 27, 34-37, 39, 43-44, 47, 155-157 (App. A)
Bird, William, 57
Black, Cathleen, 93
Boards of Directors
    composition, 42
    recommendations, 14, 142-143, 146
Bollinger, Lee, 126
Brody, Jeffrey H., 93-94
Bryan, Stewart, 65-66, 67, 71
Buffet, Warren, 65, 68, 73
Burleigh, William, 64, 65, 66, 69-70

Central Newspapers, 4, 27, 33, 34-37, 39, 43-44, 47, 157-159, (App. A)
Circulation
    efforts to increase, 96-97
    decline in, 21-22, 94-95
    importance of, 93-95
    low-income readers and, 91-94, 95-97
    of publicly owned newspaper companies, 2, 26
    of all chains, 2
    of secondary consequence, 9
    quality and, 69-70, 89-90, 97
    revenues from, 24
    shedding, 129-130
Compensation
    bonuses, 48-50, 100, 105, 113
    circulation and, 94, 95
    committees, 48-49, 52
    criteria, 51-52
    market performance and, 110-111
    of directors, 48
    reports on, 144
    stock awards, 49-52, 100-101, 105-106
Conclusions, 6-13

Dabney, Virginius, 128
Detroit Free Press, 96
Detroit News, 96
Dow Jones & Co., 4, 10, 28, 34-37, 39, 43-44, 47, 51, 160-162 (App. A)
Drewry, William, 57, 58, 61

Editorial Judgment
    technology, economics and, 115-134
Editor & Publisher, 94-95
Editors
    and budgets, 85
    bonuses for, 88-90
    on bottom-line pressure, 79-85
    on quality, 85-86
    stockholders and, 87
    stock options and, 86-88, 90
Entman, Robert, 132

Fancher, Michael R., 40, 54
Favre, Gregory, 92, 93, 97
Fine, Lauren, 57, 58, 59, 61-62

Gannett Co., 4, 28, 33, 34-37, 39, 43-44, 47, 48, 50, 57, 58, 165-167 (App. A)
Goldman, Sachs, 45
Graham, Donald, 64-65, 66, 68, 69-70, 71
Gray Communications, 4, 28-29, 34-37, 39, 43-44, 46, 47, 167-169 (App. A)
Groves, Miles E., 93

201

Gruenich, Kevin, 57, 58, 62

Hollinger International, 4, 29, 34-37, 39, 43-44, 47, 170-172 (App. A)
Hutchins Commission on Freedom of the Press, 115, 116, 121-124, 126, 127, 128, 133

Incentives, 8, 12, 101, 105, 112-113, 154
    circulation and, 94-95, 143
    for news personnel, 14, 51, 143-144
    management and directors, 14, 143-144
    quality and, 143-144
Independent Newspapers, Inc., 149
Institutional investors
    behavior of, 72-74, 110-111
    role of, 17-18

Jelenic, Robert, 64, 66, 70-71
Jinks, Larry, 42
Johnson, Tom, 41-42
Joint Operating Agreements, 147
Journal Register Co., 4, 29, 34-35, 37, 39, 43-44, 47, 172-174 (App. A)

Kann, Peter, 65, 66, 67, 68, 71-72
King, Maxwell E.P., 91-92, 93, 97
Knight Ridder, 4, 29-30, 34-36, 39, 43-44, 47, 49, 89, 174-176 (App. A)
Kupinski, Michael 57

Lee Enterprises, 4, 30, 34-37, 39, 44, 47, 177-179 (App. A)
Lord Thompson, 17
Los Angeles Times and Staples Center, 100-101

Madigan, Kenneth, 65, 66, 67, 68, 69, 71
Market segmentation, 2, 7, 9-10, 100, 107, 108, 112, 122-123, 125, 127, 128, 129, 130, 131-132, 133-134, 136, 145

McClatchy Co., 4, 10, 30, 34-36, 39, 42, 43-44, 47, 49, 50, 70, 94, 179-181 (App. A)
McCoy, Melissa, 54
Media General, 4, 30-31, 34-37, 39, 43-44, 47, 182-184 (App. A)
Milwaukee Journal, 97
Morgan, J. P., 45

Naughton, James, 78, 90
Neuharth, Al, 96
New London Day, 150
New York Times Co., 4, 10, 31, 34-37, 39, 43-44, 47, 50, 51, 63, 88, 184-186 (App. A)
News
    as business commodity, 1-2, 9, 108-109, 154
    as instrument for advertising, 110, 131
    consequences for, 12
    fragmented audience for, 108-109
    judgment, 115-134
    trends in, 141
    wall between business and, 99-100
Newspaper Association of America, 92-93, 97
Newspaper CEOs
    views of, 64-72, 74-75
The Newspaper Publishing Industry, 94
Newspapers, publicly traded
    boards of directors, 42
    circulation, 26
    classes of stock, 43-44
    economic performance, 18, 33-39
    forces for change, 113-134
    number, 25
    organization, 101-113
    ownership by institutions, 45-46, 47
    profit maximization and, 108-109
    profit strategy, 139-140
    revenues, 26
    role of advertisers, 107, 112
    role of families, 45-46
Newspapers

number, 18-19
    forms of ownership, 148-152
    government policy toward, 146-148
    role of technology, economics, 115-134

Office of Drug Policy, 101
Operating margins, 9-10, 18, 33, 111
Overholser, Geneva, 90-91

Pagination, 53-55
People's Charter Union, 118
Picard, Robert G., 93-94
Philadelphia Inquirer, 56, 57, 91
Postman, Neil, 125
Profits
    disclosure of, 144-145
    role of, 17, 98-100
Project for Excellence in Journalism, 6
Pruitt, Gary B., 42, 64, 65, 66, 68, 70, 94
Pulitzer Publishing, 4, 31, 44, 47, 187-188 (App. A)

Readership
    daily and Sunday, 23
    defined, 21
    demographics of, 23
    importance of, 94-95
    loss of, 22-23, 94-95
    stress on upscale, 25, 91-96, 99-100
Recommendations, 14-15, 141-153
Ridder, Anthony, 58, 65, 67, 71
Roberts, Gene, 56-57
Rowe, Sandra M., 40, 41-42, 95
Russial, John, 53

E.W. Scripps Co., 4, 28, 34-37, 39, 43-44, 46, 47, 162-165 (App. A)
Squires, James, 92-93, 97
St. Petersburg Times, 96-97, 149-150
Stamp Act, 1, 118
"The State of the American Newspaper", 5-6
State Street Corp., 45
Stock analysts
    influence of, 74
    role of, 56-57
    views of, 58-64
Stock market
    distorting effect, 7
    influence of, 105-106
    investor objectives, 8
    marketplace of ideas and, 139
    pressures, 11
    return on investment, 36
    short-term orientation, 7, 105, 106
Stock options or awards, 49-52, 86-88, 90, 100-101, 105-106
Stock price
    attention to, 67-69
    effect on newsrooms, 84-85
    increase in, 35

Tax and securities laws
    changes, 14-15
    holding period for capital gains, 145-146
    Internal Revenue Code section 162(m), 52
    non-profit news organizations, 148-152
    SEC rules on Communication, 73-74, 152-153
Times Mirror Co., 4, 32, 33, 34-36, 39, 43-44, 47, 188-190 (App. A)
Time Warner, 60
Tribune Co., 4, 31-32, 34-37, 39, 44, 47, 191-193 (App. A)

U.S. Supreme Court, 1, 138-139

Warburg, Pincus, 43
Washington Post Co., 4, 10, 32, 34-37, 39, 43-44, 47, 48, 63, 193-196 (App. A)
Weil III, Louis A., 64, 65, 67, 68-69, 71
Wellington Management, 45
White, William Allen, 127
Willes, Mark, 78, 97
Winter, Mary Ann, 57, 58, 61
Woodworth, Robert, 65, 67, 69, 71

ISBN 0-8138-2459-1

PN 4888.O85 C73 2001